MODELLING NAVAL SHIPS
IN SMALL SCALES

MODELLING NAVAL SHIPS

IN SMALL SCALES

Mike McCabe

THE CROWOOD PRESS

First published in 2021 by
The Crowood Press Ltd
Ramsbury, Marlborough
Wiltshire SN8 2HR

enquiries@crowood.com

This impression 2022

www.crowood.com

British Library Cataloguing-in-Publication Data
A catalogue record for this book is available from the British Library.

ISBN 978 1 78500 850 4

Dedication and Acknowledgements

This book is dedicated to the two most important women in my life: my wife Jill, for her support and patience during its writing; and my sister Ceri, who passed away as it was nearing completion. Thanks also to friends who both helped out and provided moral support, particularly Malcolm Finch, Paul Rowlands and Barry Spencer; but also many more with whom I have talked about modelling over the years, who have shared tips and provided inspiration to me to keep trying to do better.

Typeset by Simon and Sons
Cover design by Blue Sunflower Creative
Printed and bound in India by Parksons Graphics Pvt Ltd

Contents

Introduction

Ships are one of the very oldest forms of transport, so of course ship models have been around for a very long time. They are the classic model, having style, grace and presence so perfect as a centrepiece. Where there is a history of ship building, museums hold builders' models made by craftsmen and apprentices to show their skills and those of the ship workers, and the pride that has been taken in them is there for all to see. At home, a ship model makes a fine display piece for friends and family to admire the skill of the maker. Ships are individuals, they have names, histories and stories. They are entwined with the lives of the crew and passengers, and for many they have been home.

There are many reasons to want to build model ships: to remember a career at sea, a relation who served, to recall history, or simply the pleasure of building a beautiful and intricate model. Whatever the reason, model ships of all types are a challenge for the modeller as they demand a range of skills: accuracy in building, neatness in painting, a steady hand for rigging, and an artist's eye for creating realistic water. For such large vessels to be a reasonably sized model they are often by necessity built in much smaller scales than other types of model. Photoetched parts to produce very fine detail are common and require some delicacy, while resin kits are a common choice rather than rare diversion. Building ship models is probably the most difficult of all types of modelling, but it is also the most rewarding.

In recent years there has been a great increase in the number and variety of kits and accessories available, along with the number of companies producing them. The rise of 3D design and printing has helped to fuel this, and with greater availability of subjects comes an increase in interest. Although ships still form a relatively small proportion of the completed models seen at local and national shows, this is certainly increasing and the number willing to try their hand is undoubtedly growing. For those brought up for many years on the limited range on offer from brands such as Airfix, Revell and Heller, to see a French pre-dreadnought battleship or an Italian heavy cruiser available as a kit from mainstream plastic kit manufacturers is quite remarkable.

Over the length of time ships have been built they have been put to a countless variety of uses. Modelling them varies widely in scale, function and materials, and they may be static models or designed to be able to float and operated by radio control. Such a wide range of model styles would be impossible to cover in one book, and that is not the aim. This book concentrates on plastic and resin kits in the most common scales of 1/700 and 1/350, and by personal preference in a waterline style with a seascape base. This is not to say that many of the techniques do not apply to larger and smaller scales and other styles of model: they most certainly do.

Similarly, building ship models encompasses a great number of skills and techniques that it is not possible to cover in one volume. Here the most commonly used will be described as they relate to the subjects being built. No doubt you will have your own views on some of the techniques and will prefer to do some things differently; developing your own methods and personal style is a great thing, as it will bring an individuality to your finished models. Do not be afraid to experiment, and to adapt a model to your own particular needs and abilities.

The modelling hobby as a whole has seen a boom in the numbers of painting and weathering products available. Partly this is due to the much greater number of kits and accessories now available, which has led the focus of the modeller away from scratch building their own parts or even complete models, and more towards painting and finishing. A downside to this is that this great variety of paints, washes and powders can become confusing, especially when so many magazines and websites appear devoted to promoting one brand or another as though no model can be considered complete without them.

The techniques shown in this book do at times recommend products, but bear in mind that on the whole these are all basically well known and used types: oil-based enamels and artist oils, water-based acrylics, pastels for powders. In fact the majority of weathering products are formulations of these basic materials, and thinned, mixed or ground ready for use. For that reason this book will show how to use the types of material, since understanding how they work will then leave the choice of personal brand preference to the modeller.

Hopefully this book will act as part guide, part inspiration to you as modeller to use some of the techniques yourself and to develop your own. There is no substitute for trying, learning, then mastering new skills and gaining confidence in your modelling. Building model ships is challenging, addictive, fascinating, so let us dive into this hugely enjoyable hobby.

Chapter One

Where Do I Start?

THE SCALE QUESTION

Early Days: 1/600 Scale

For most of us in the UK the first ship model we built was probably from the Airfix range of 1/600 scale kits dating back to the early 1960s. Still popular with many modellers in this country, it has unfortunately been rather left behind as the most commonly used scale for ship models. As a result very few new kits have been issued in 1/600 since the early 1980s; nevertheless the nostalgia value of building something with the wonderful Airfix Roy Cross box art still holds a strong appeal for many who also prefer the slightly larger size of parts over the much more common smaller ship 1/700 scale. This was the chosen scale for a series of kits produced by four Japanese companies in the 1970s, who joined forces with the aim of between them making a kit of every World War II Imperial Japanese Navy ship available.

Why 1/700 was chosen isn't particularly clear, but as a result of the number of kits released and the improvement in quality of most of these over the older Airfix catalogue, this gradually became the standard for smaller scale. For those with limited room for display it is an ideal size, since it provides a good compromise between the amount of shelf space required and the level of detail that can be packed into a model. An average battleship model in 1/700 would be around 25–30cm in length.

1/700 Scale

As the standard scale for ships, there is a huge choice in 1/700, covering just about every period and type. Of course the incredible variety of ships

Just a tiny part of the massive range of subjects available in 1/700 scale. Many subjects previously only available in resin are now being produced in injection plastic because Chinese manufacturers such as Trumpeter and Flyhawk have started to release kits.

built over the centuries means that there is still a great number of vessels for which there is nothing currently available in kit form. If you are looking for anything from a World War II battleship to a Finnish coastal defence ship or a Peruvian monitor, then 1/700 scale is for you, although the larger scales are quickly catching up in terms of the number of subjects available. Despite the increase in popularity of larger models, a trend generally reflected across the modelling world as a whole, there are no signs that 1/700 as the standard scale for ships is likely to change at any time in the near future.

1/350 Scale

For many of us, advancing years means that eyesight becomes less sharp and hands rather less steady, so something a little larger is less of a challenge. Not too long after releasing their range of 1/700 kits, Tamiya of Japan brought out a number of battleship kits twice the size, in 1/350 scale. For a number of years it seemed as though this was not to be very popular with modellers, as the number of plastic kits added to these first few releases was a long time coming. But this has all changed within the last couple of decades, as the scale has seen a surge in popularity, initially mainly by resin producers, but then taken up largely by the Chinese company Trumpeter, which at the time of writing has released almost 100 kits in 1/350 scale.

Other manufacturers have followed this lead, and the larger, more impressive size of these models, combined with the increase in subject examples and the availability of accessories, means that this is now the scale of choice for a large proportion of ship modellers. The downside is, of course, that the increased size of a 1/350 model requires four times the shelf space than a 1/700 model does, since it is twice the length and twice the width. Often people say that it is easier to build in 1/350 as the parts are much larger, although one thing to consider is that as the scale is larger, so detail that would be hinted at or missed off altogether in 1/700 may need to be included in 1/350. Small details such as handwheels, hatch covers and cable reels could all be omitted from a smaller-scale model without drawing any attention, but if not included in a larger scale might lead to a model starting to look a little bare. Of course it is the level of complexity of subject that makes ships such a fascinating topic to model.

The larger scale 1/350 is becoming more popular, both leading to and being driven by a lot of new releases in injection plastic. Hobby Boss in particular has some very interesting and unusual kits in their continually expanding range.

1/200 Scale

The year 2009 saw the release by Trumpeter of the first in a range of 1/200 scale ships, a development very much in line with the generally increased size of model kits. This certainly makes for large and impressive models: a 1/200 model of HMS *Hood* is over 1.3 *metres* in length, with a corresponding increase in the level of detail. This does come at some cost, of course, especially if aftermarket photo-etched brass and resin upgrade sets are to be added. If the space is available to store such a museum-sized model, it would be sure to make a very impressive centrepiece. Although this would seem to be an ideal scale for smaller subjects, giving a very good balance between size and level of detail, kit releases at least so far have concentrated on battleship-sized models; it would therefore be good to see this scale develop with some less space-demanding models becoming available.

Other Scales

There are, of course, a great many other kits available in a myriad of scales: 1/400 is the European equivalent of 1/600 in the UK, and the French company Heller continues to produce kits in this scale, as do a few other plastic and resin companies. For those wanting something smaller, 1/1200 is popular with collectors, and this is mostly concentrated on merchant shipping, with some very nicely detailed models available. Rather than list everything available, for the purposes of this book we will concentrate on the two most popular scales of 1/700 and 1/350, as this is where the majority of ship modellers will be working.

THREE METHODS OF KIT PRODUCTION

Injection Plastic Kits

By far the most common and familiar to most modellers is the injection plastic kit. These may be anything from a large manufacturer such as Tamiya of Japan producing thousands of kits of a release in a single production run, down to small companies where a limited run of a few hundred is made. Simply put, injection kits are made by first creating a mould: this is usually metal, and is either machined or created by using electrical discharge to create the desired shapes, although increasingly this is being done by using 3D printed polymers designed by CAD (computer-aided design). Plastic beads are then heated and injected into the mould under pressure to produce the kit parts, once these are sufficiently cooled. This process produces parts attached to a plastic framework, the 'sprue', from which the parts need to be cut.

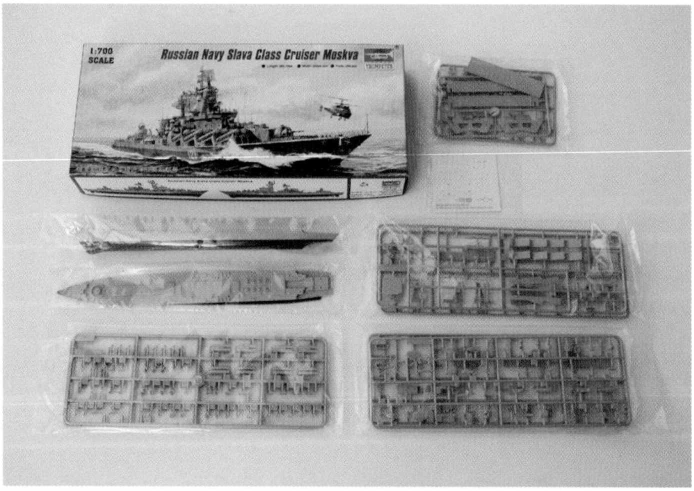

A typical modern injection plastic kit, in this case the Trumpeter 1/700 model of the Slava-class cruiser Moskva.

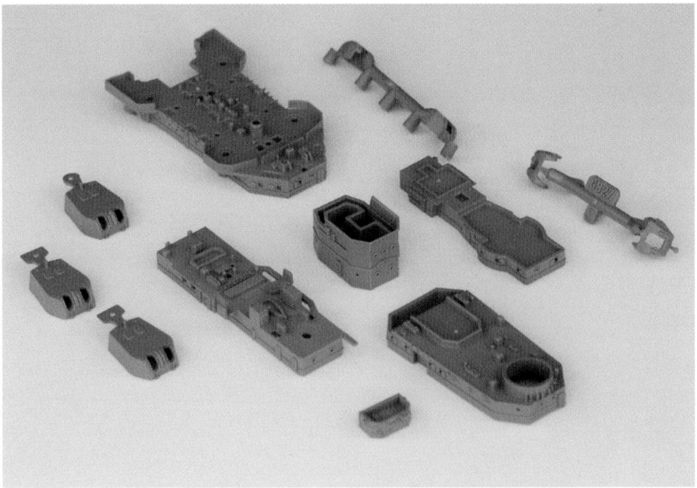

An example of the level of detail that can be achieved with modern slide-moulding technology; this is from the kit for the Flyhawk 1/700 model of HMS Aurora.

The process of manufacturing the mould is the most expensive part of this process and can cost many thousands of pounds, although the sprue of kit parts itself will cost just a few pence. For this reason injection plastic kits require a very significant start-up cost, even for limited run items. Advances in moulding technology since the turn of the century have led to what is known as 'slide moulding': this allows moulds to be built in many parts, which then slide together to form the complete mould, rather than being a simple sandwich of two halves. This means that more complex shapes can be produced and in much greater levels of detail. The Chinese company Flyhawk has proved the most successful at exploiting this method, and produces some very high quality kits with a level of detail not previously seen in injection moulding.

The advantages of injection-moulded kits are simply that there are many more of them, and they are cheaper on the whole than resin alternatives. Initially in terms of our focus on scales, as most of the early kits came from Japanese manufacturers, there was not surprisingly a concentration on Imperial Japanese Navy subjects from World War II. A few Royal Navy, US Navy and German Kriegsmarine kits came along later. Since 2005 there has been a significant expansion of choice, especially from the Chinese company Trumpeter and their sister Hobby Boss, who have taken on some very interesting and totally unexpected subjects. That it is now possible to have a 1/350 French pre-dreadnought battleship in injection plastic is something that even ten years ago would have seemed like wish-listing in the extreme, but with three such kits released in 2017 it is surely a sign that interest in ship modelling is growing.

Resin Kits

The second most common method for making kits is resin casting. This process involves creating a master pattern either by hand or, more commonly these days, by CAD design, then 3D printing. This is then used as the basis for casting the kit parts. The parts are put into a mould of silicon RTV (room temperature vulcanization) rubber, with a hardening agent that causes the liquid rubber to harden over a period of hours to produce a stiff yet still flexible mould that is capable of picking up extremely fine detail. A two-part polyurethane resin is then poured into the mould, often with a dye to give a grey finish; this is then usually placed in a vacuum chamber to ensure that air is forced out of the mould, and the resin occupies the spaces to create an exact likeness.

This is, of course, a much simplified version of the process, but the basic principle applies regardless of the techniques and equipment used. On

Some resin kits from a variety of manufacturers in both 1/700 and 1/350 scale.

the whole, resin casting is carried out by smaller companies with much shorter production runs, as each mould will generally last for only twenty-five to thirty copies of a kit before requiring replacement.

Resin kits are normally more expensive than plastic due to the cost of making the master pattern, which has to be spread over a far shorter production run, and the relatively much higher cost of materials per kit compared to injection plastic processes. Where this has been produced by CAD and 3D printing, design time is the most costly part of the process. As a means of creating kits of more unusual subjects, resin is far more common as a medium for ship modelling than, say, aircraft or armour, and it is well worthwhile learning the slightly different techniques for building a resin model, as it will open up a huge range of possibilities.

Most modern resin kits are more complete than their plastic counterparts; etched brass is almost standard, with turned brass, especially for the larger scale, becoming increasingly common. Detail is also often superior, although injection-plastic techniques employed by some companies are starting to approach even the quality of the best resin kits. More commonly the reason modellers give for not wanting to work with resin is the cost, and the fear that their skills will not be up to the task and they will have wasted money on a kit they have not been able to complete. However, there are very many small kits in resin that make ideal subjects to learn the basic techniques and overcome those fears. The better resin kits are, if anything, easier to build than plastic kits, since CAD design allows for an excellent fit of parts and the best castings need very little in the way of cleaning up. Once you take the plunge and start building in resin, there is a world of possibility in front of you.

3D Printing

A few short years ago this summary on how kits are produced would have stopped at the first two sections, but as ever technology is advancing, and we are now only at the start of the potential revolution in the hobby that 3D design and printing is likely to bring. Put very simply, 3D printing or 'additive manufacturing' (AM) is the process where a design is made on a computer using CAD software, then downloaded to a printer which, using a plastic polymer, gradually builds up layers to create the finished object. Both the type of material used and the quality of the printer, in terms of the fineness of the printed layer, will determine the eventual quality of the finished object.

Cheaper machines will produce a coarse and grainy product with visible lines, particularly on rounded surfaces, while the hard nature of the material means that these are very difficult to sand and remove. In contrast, a high quality machine will produce an object with very little visible deformation. Towards the end of the 2010s the production of such high quality end-products requires a considerable outlay, although this is a rapidly developing technology – perhaps we will see a high quality 3D printer as an everyday object within the next decade.

Producing a high quality original as far as possible free of obvious printing lines is not cheap, so this is generally used as the basis for resin casting once it is cleaned up. At present this is the main use of 3D printing, other than for some small accessories. Where it is used through market places such as Shapeways for kits, they are generally very expensive and not in my experience very high quality, although this is improving and will no doubt become considerably better in future. It is certainly interesting to wonder where this technology will lead us, as it has the potential to completely change so many aspects of our lives.

ACCESSORIES

Photoetched Brass

The development of parts made from photoetched brass is a revelation to many modellers in terms of the level of intricacy and detail it can bring to a model. Previously some method of replicating open platform supports, lattice towers and the like with sprue or painting techniques was the only way to achieve this. With photoetch, fine details can be added to bring the necessary complexity to the model, and using it will allow a level of finesse not easily available through any other means.

It could be argued with some justification that especially in small scales, items such as railings are overscale. However, missing these details off entirely can make the model look over-simplified, so it is a matter of individual choice whether to include them or not. For myself, the attraction for building ship models is the visual complexity of the subject, so adding photoetched details greatly increases this and makes the model look 'busy' and more like the real thing.

Possibly more than any other type of modelling, the use of photoetch as required has become the standard for ship models; some plastic kits will include a small fret for parts such as cranes and catapults, which have an open lattice structure. Although it may seem difficult and demanding at first, it is well worth learning to work with photoetched parts and gaining confidence in their regular use, as it will bring a great improvement in the quality of the finished model.

Photoetched parts – or just 'etch', as it is more commonly known – is usually made from thin sheets of brass of 0.1mm thickness as standard, though sometimes the slightly stiffer nickel silver or much harder stainless steel is also used. Thicker materials may be used as needed, particularly for larger scales and larger parts, where both the increased strength and scale thickness are an

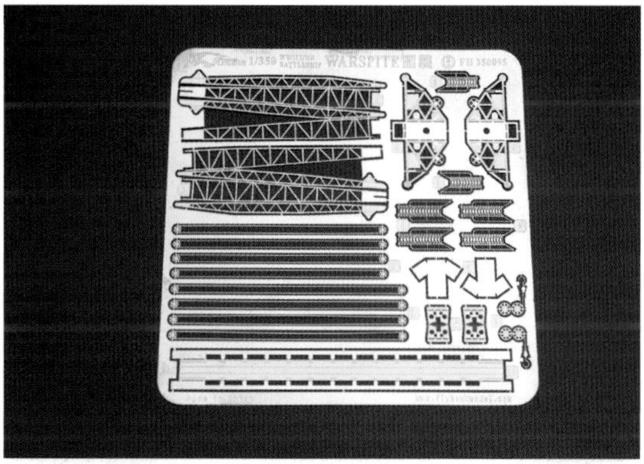

Etched brass from the Flyhawk 1/350 upgrade set for the Academy model of HMS Warspite. *Cranes are a good example of where etched brass is a superior choice for finely detailed parts.*

advantage. As with 3D-printed parts, CAD is also used to create the design, although previously this was done laboriously by hand. This is then printed on to a negative sheet for both sides of the design, and treated with acid to remove the areas of metal not required.

The end product is a thin sheet with the parts marked out (the fret) and connected to the framework with small tags. These parts are then cut away from the framework and either used as they are if needed flat, or bent into three-dimensional shapes. A huge variety of etched brass sets can be found: some are of the generic type of individual sets of railings, doors, cable reels and similar, while others are tailored to individual kits to provide all the parts needed to upgrade the basic offering.

Aftermarket Resin

'Aftermarket' is the term used to describe any accessory made to add detail to a basic kit, whether etched brass, resin, wooden decks or any such improvement in detail. A number of companies specialize in producing these parts, with resin being the most commonly used, alongside etched brass. These mainly feature details that are not well realized in plastic kits, especially weapons and mounts, boats, aircraft, anchors, winches and many others commonly found in aftermarket sets.

Aftermarket sets are a small and inexpensive way to improve a basic kit, although the more involved sets that include resin, etched brass and turned brass parts are of course a little more expensive. Some excellent detail parts are made by 3D printing, where the small size of many of these makes it cost effective to produce sets directly produced by this method.

Wooden Decks

Another relatively new accessory is in the form of laser-cut wooden decks. Very thin sheets of wood are cut by laser to fit a particular kit accurately and so give the impression of a wooden deck. These are backed by adhesive so they can be placed directly on to the kit deck, often accompanied by an identically cut masking sheet that can be used to paint the rest of the model once the deck is attached. The idea of wooden decks is that the natural colour and grain of the material will replicate the wooden deck sections on the model without the need to paint. Of course the grain of the wood is 1:1 scale, whilst due to the type of wood used, the colour tends towards yellow, whereas ship decks, which are normally made of teak, fade towards a mid-grey colour.

Finally there is the issue that even for the thinnest of wooden decks, there will be a step between planked and steel areas on the model due to the thickness of the material; also some height of the superstructures and deck fittings will be lost for the same reason. However, a lot of modellers do enjoy using these, and as with everything in modelling and life, it is a matter of opinion and personal taste.

Aftermarket AA weapons in 1/350 scale from the Veteran range; these include resin, photoetch and turned brass barrels for a very detailed result.

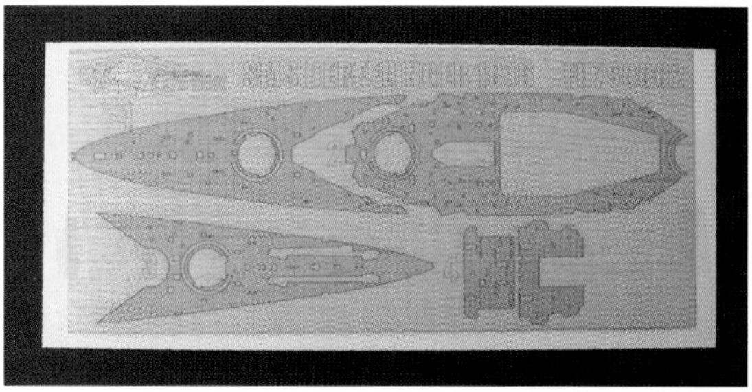

A replacement wooden deck; this is for the Flyhawk 1/700 model of the German battlecruiser Derfflinger.

Turned Brass and Other Accessories

One relatively inexpensive way of improving any warship model is to use turned-metal gun barrels. Weapons are always a feature of any military model, and this is no less true for model warships. Due to the limitations of injection plastic and resin casting, there are often imperfections on kit barrels due to seam lines, offsetting on both sides, or a bend in the plastic that is difficult to correct. Turned brass is commonly used for smaller barrels, along with aluminium for 1/350 scale replacements. Metal cut by computer-controlled lathes has the advantage of being able to reproduce a perfectly round cross-section, with the details of flared and hollowed-out muzzles helping to make such a difference in detail.

Many options for turned brass barrels are available, including for light anti-aircraft weapons, and full sets to cover all the varying calibres required on specific ship models. Another very useful accessory along the same lines is turned-brass tapered masts; we shall see the advantage of these in the rigging chapter.

To make a full list of the huge variety of aftermarket details available would be difficult, but looking through the items offered by any specialist ship-model retailer will bring up scale chain, crew figures, aircraft weapons, rigging material, decals, paper flags and much more. It is a good bet that if you can think of something that would enhance your model, so has somebody else already, and you will be able to find it somewhere. If not, then get in touch with one of them to suggest it.

Upgrade Sets

For many of the more popular kits, complete upgrade sets are available that will include at least one, but more often more, of the types of aftermarket parts mentioned. Some of these are extremely complex and quite expensive, usually costing more than the kit they are intended to detail. They do, however, provide a package that will go a very long way towards allowing the modeller to produce a highly detailed model of their chosen subject. Commonly one of these sets will include etched brass, resin replacement parts and turned brass barrels and other details, with wooden decks becoming more frequent. Unless you have a large spares box with a lot of etched brass frets and resin replacements, these can prove to be quite a cost-effective way of getting all the parts needed to bring your model to another level.

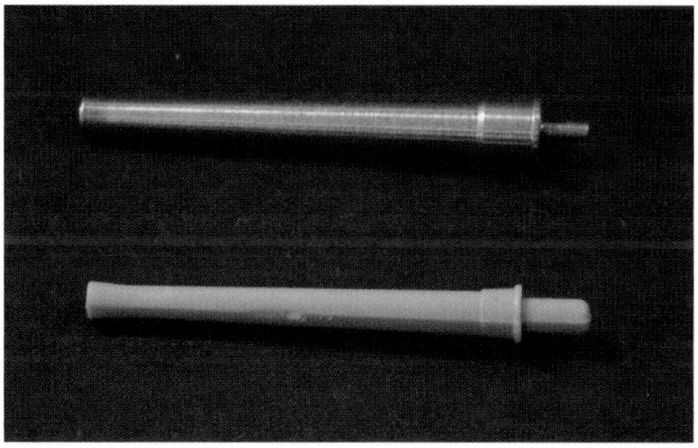

Turned brass barrels compared to the plastic version; notice that the plastic part has a seam, and often the plastic part is offset.

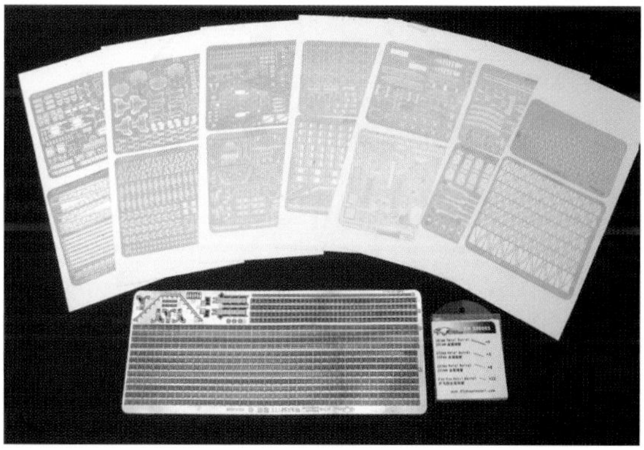

Upgrade set; this is the Flyhawk 1/350 set for the Academy model of HMS Warspite.

WATERLINE AND FULL HULL

Simply put, most 1/700 kits come as waterline kits, and most 1/350 kits have a full hull option. The choice of which to model is, of course, entirely up to the individual, although if you prefer full hull and want to model in 1/700, you will find your choices limited unless you are prepared to make the part of the hull under the waterline yourself. All is not lost, though, as many of the later Trumpeter releases do indeed have a full hull option. It is, of course, much simpler in 1/350 to remove the lower hull to make a waterline model. As someone who likes the challenge of making a realistic seabase, and as I like to make a ship in its natural element, I prefer waterline, so the models in this book will be built in that way. Largely, though, it is a matter of whether the modeller prefers to build a waterline model with weathering and perhaps crew on a seabase, or a museum-type build to show the lines of the ship and keep the build as clean as possible.

Both styles can produce very fine models, and neither should be considered to take precedence over the other, although personally I find that a model built with weathering, figures or in action and then placed full hull on a pedestal just does not look right. An advantage for the waterline builder in possession of a kit that is full hull is that a little of the lower hull can be shown on the seabase. This can make for a very nice effect, showing the ship pitching and rolling in heavier seas, greatly adding to the realism of the finished model.

Putting it all together results in an impressive model, such as this 1/350 model of HMS Sheffield *built from a resin kit with some extras.*

Chapter Two

Tools and Equipment

Starting to build model ships does not need any great outlay, as modelling can begin with a small set of tools. As with other types of modelling, requirements are for cutting, filling, sanding and gluing, although with much of the work involving small and delicate parts, some optical assistance is likely to be needed for many modellers. Painting will be covered in a separate chapter, so the equipment relating to that will be explored in full later in the book.

CUTTING TOOLS

Cutting tools are needed to remove parts from the kit sprues, for altering details and to scrape away seam marks. For larger parts sprue cutters are very useful: these are spring-loaded tools with the cutting edge along one side so you can get close in to the part. There are many makes of these; those made by Tamiya are well made and popular, and will last a very long time if used properly. Don't be tempted to cut metal rod or other hard items with these as it will damage the cutting edges.

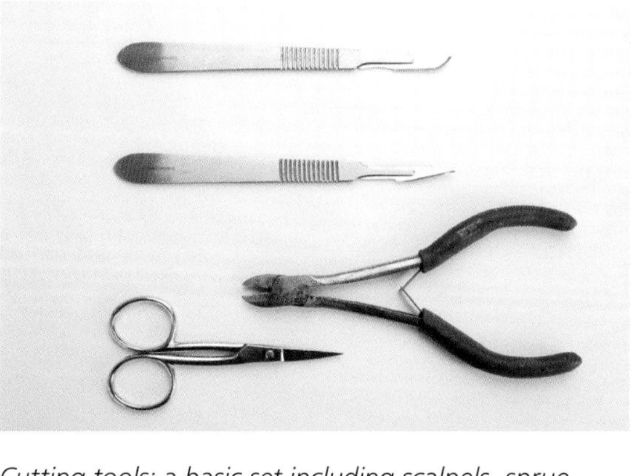

Cutting tools: a basic set including scalpels, sprue cutter and nail scissors – the latter with curved blades is very useful for trimming photoetch.

For cutting small parts from sprues and resin runners a scalpel is the best tool. Swann Morton make many types of blade with a slim metal handle that fits all of these. For general use a No. 11 blade is ideal: this is a long, triangular blade that comes to a point and is excellent for cutting away small parts and for general use. The flat edge of the blade is very useful for scraping away seam lines and unwanted plastic. For cutting etched brass parts and plastic card, a round-edged No. 10 blade is best as it will not dig into the area to be cut in the same way as a pointed blade.

Care needs to be taken with all blade edges, of course, but particularly with scalpel blades, which are extremely sharp. They are also thin and can be quite brittle, so care is needed when cutting thick plastic in case the blade shatters. It is best to cut out thicker parts in sections rather than trying to force the blade through in one go. Change the blades regularly as a sharp blade is actually safer than a blunt one – the temptation when using a blunt blade is to force the cut, making it much more likely that it will slip and cause injury. It is cheaper in the longer term to buy blades in bulk; packs of 100 Swann Morton blades can be bought at around £10, so a fresh blade is always on hand.

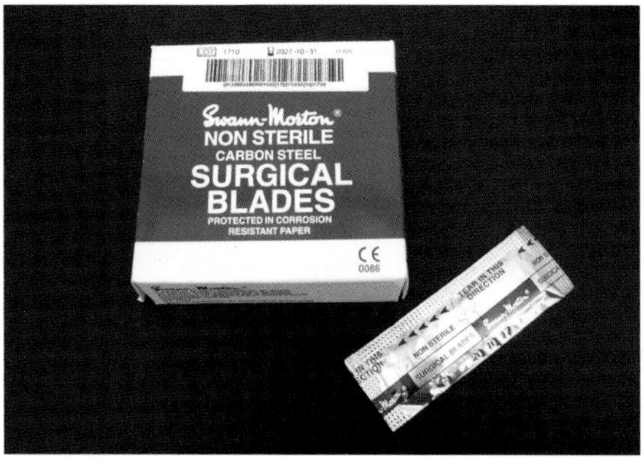

Scalpel blades are much cheaper when bought in bulk; keep an old blade for applying filler to small areas and similar jobs.

A set of micro-drill bits and a small hand-pin vice are very useful for opening up portholes and gun barrels and for cleaning up location points, and for many other uses. These can be bought from any good model shop, though care needs to be taken in particular with the very small drill bits as they are fragile and can snap, especially if the hole drilled is too deep.

The last part of the basic cutting kit is a good pair of sharp nail scissors; these can be used for trimming etch parts, and have many other uses. Once the edge goes from these they can be used for cutting metal rod.

Helpful Hint

I use wooden toothpicks a lot during modelling: they are ideal for getting small dabs of glue into the exact place, and can be sharpened further when a very small amount is needed.

FILLING AND SANDING

Even the best kit will not fit exactly or will require some removal of the attachment point for parts, so some means of filling and sanding will be necessary. Having said that, the best way to avoid using filler is to test-fit and work on the parts as far as possible to ensure the best fit before gluing into place. This will avoid the overuse of filler and any attendant problems it may cause.

For sanding at its simplest, various grades of wet-and-dry paper bought inexpensively from Halfords the car suppliers are sufficient for many jobs. These sheets can be cut into smaller pieces, wrapped around wooden sticks, or taped to the cutting mat for sanding bases flat; they are generally versatile enough for most jobs, given the different grades. When sanding resin parts there is the additional benefit that they can be used with a small amount of water to reduce the amount of potentially harmful resin dust produced.

Other than wet-and-dry paper, sanding sticks are very useful: they can be found in packs of different grades, and in widths of around 3mm, ideal for the small areas found on most small-scale ships. Round plastic needle files are also handy for getting into angles and curves.

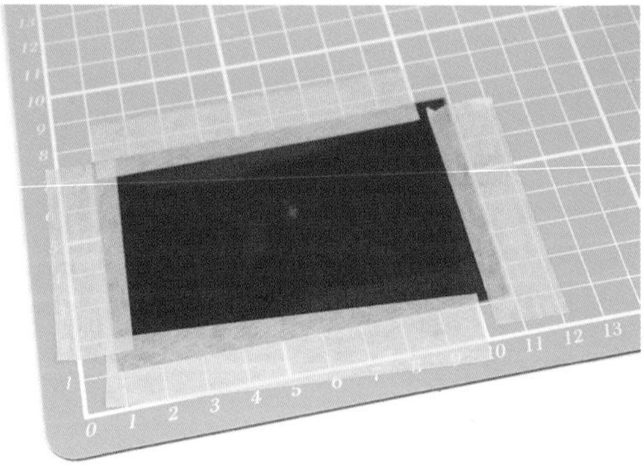

Taping some wet and dry paper to the corner of the cutting mat is a good way of sanding parts flat.

Sanding sticks are very useful for cleaning up parts, and can easily be kept at hand on the workbench.

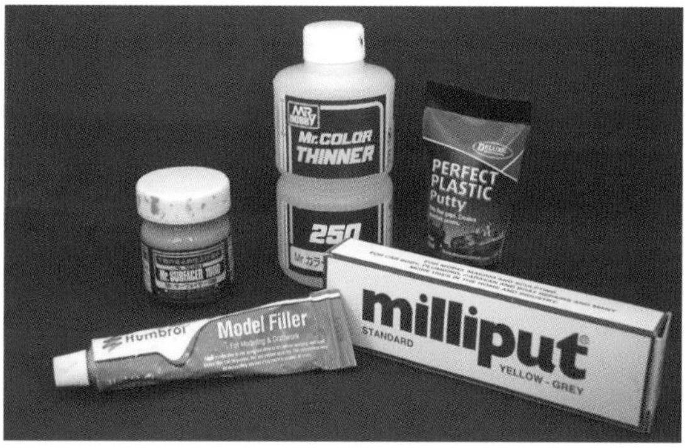

Fillers of various grades from Milliput for large gaps and shaping of parts, to Mr Surfacer for very fine holes or scratches.

Unless the sanding job needed is a very heavy one, metal files will generally be far too coarse to be of much use on plastic or resin, though they are, of course, fine for brass rod or similar thick metal parts. It is very easy to overdo the use of a metal file and scratch the surface of the model, so causing more damage than the job might have entailed in the first place. Use of these should be reserved for opening up apertures or similar heavy-duty work.

There are many types of filler on the market; all have their different strengths and weaknesses, and can be used in a variety of situations – but at the moment there is no such thing as the perfect filler for all situations. Rarely is there much use for the putty type of fillers such as Milliput, as most filling work will be in the form of very small gaps in between superstructure parts and the deck, or similar.

The Mr Surfacer range of liquid fillers comes in very useful for such tasks. These are cellulose-based thinners that are available in various thicknesses, although as they tend to last a long time, the thickness becomes less accurate as they become more and more viscous with age. They can be freshened up by the addition of cellulose thinners, so although quite expensive, they do have a very long shelf life. The great advantage of this range is that when used with their own brand, Mr Thinner, they can be painted on to the gap to be filled with an old brush and then given ten minutes or so to dry; the excess is then removed by a cotton bud soaked in thinner, so leaving a very neat fill without any need for sanding. At its thinnest 1500 grade, Mr Surfacer can be used as a primer and micro-filler when applied with an airbrush.

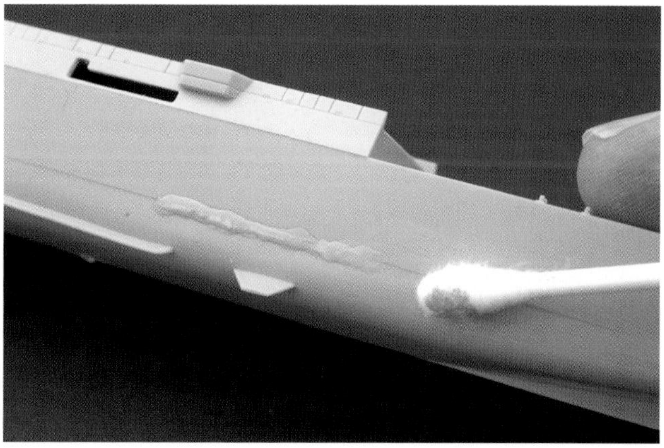

Use Mr Surfacer on a seam by placing it with a cocktail stick or similar, then soak a cotton bud in Mr Colour Thinner and wipe off the excess.

For larger gaps it is almost a matter of preference what is used, whether water-based acrylic fillers such as the Vallejo brand, the well-known Green Stuff, or for plastic the venerable Humbrol filler (essentially kit styrene dissolved in solvent). However, it is good practice to try to make sure that reaching for the filler tube or bottle is the last resort, since time spent on ensuring as good a fit as possible is better than trying to plug any gaps with filler.

ADHESIVES

For those of us of a certain age there is surely nothing more nostalgic than the smell of plastic cement and Humbrol gloss paint. Those little white and blue tubes of Airfix plastic cement have long gone, but the same basic product remains very much in use for injection plastic kits. These days it can be found in the Revell Contacta bottles, complete with a metal-tube applicator, and much easier to use.

Where two surfaces need to be joined, it may be easier to use a liquid cement such as Tamiya's liquid cement or its stronger cousin Mek Pak. Both of these adhesives are near the consistency of water, so when applied with an old brush will flow very well into the parts to be joined through capillary action. Be aware, though, that the Mek Pak bottles in particular can be easily knocked over and will create a terrible mess, so it is strongly advisable to have some form of stand to prevent this happening.

For basic plastic kit construction, this is all that is really required, as all these adhesives act by partially dissolving the plastic to create a very strong bond; they take some time to set, so parts can be adjusted. This may mean that some form of clamping is required during setting time.

Resin will not respond to styrene cements so another option is required, most usually cyanocryolate (CA) or superglue. These adhesives act by bonding to the surface of a part, so forming a very strong join; they also have the benefit of acting to some extent as a filler. Some manufacturers have sought to take advantage of this property with 'gap-filling' products, the disadvantage being that the CA bond is much harder than any surrounding plastic or resin – so smoothing down the filler, if done without care, can result in unwanted removal of the area around the join. Gap-filling CA is at the thick end of the scale, which goes down to thin adhesives with almost water-like consistency.

CA also varies in quality: the cheap tubes found in packs in DIY shops do not have the same adhesive properties as name brands, but can be useful when only small amounts are required. Quite often

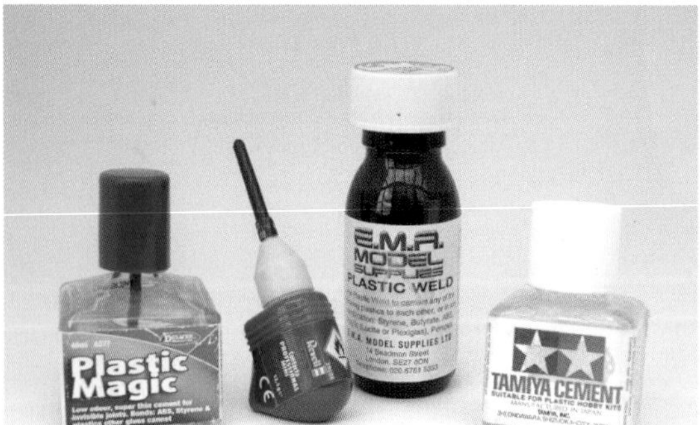

Adhesives for plastic kits with a range of thicknesses: the thinner it is, the quicker it will evaporate from the part.

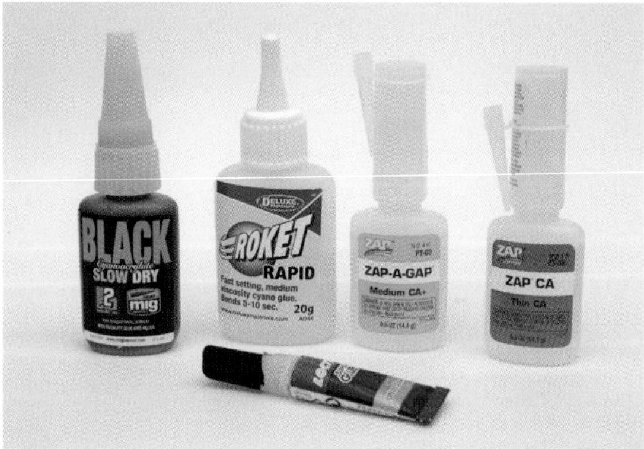

Types of CA adhesive; there are many brands available, but having a fresh supply of a cheaper alternative is often the best choice.

the freshness of CA is important: a bottle that has been open for a period of more than a couple of weeks will start to lose its strength, which can be very frustrating and messy. In general, a good quality named brand in small bottles or tubes is the best option.

One disadvantage for modellers using CA is that the bond is almost immediate, so there is very little time for adjustment, as there is with plastic kits. Where accuracy of alignment is vital, such as in the placement of superstructure parts, it can be difficult to adjust a poorly placed part, as removing it may lead to damage; certainly there will be adhesive residue that will need to be cleaned off before attempting to reposition the part. In this situation, it may be better to use a fast-setting two-part epoxy adhesive. These can be mixed in small amounts, and brands can be found that will give a five-minute setting time, long enough to give plenty of time for adjustment, but quick enough not to delay progress on the model. Of course the setting time means that parts will need to be held in place until the adhesive has fully set, which means it is not ideal for all situations.

Another extremely useful adhesive is PVA or white glue, which has many other uses; these will be discussed more fully later in the book. Micro Kristal Klear is a quality PVA glue that can be used as an adhesive for photoetch, especially when thinned with a little water. It doesn't form a strong bond, but is sufficient for etched parts. Gloss varnish can be very useful at times, especially for very small parts; it should be left for a few minutes to go tacky before use, then used as any other adhesive.

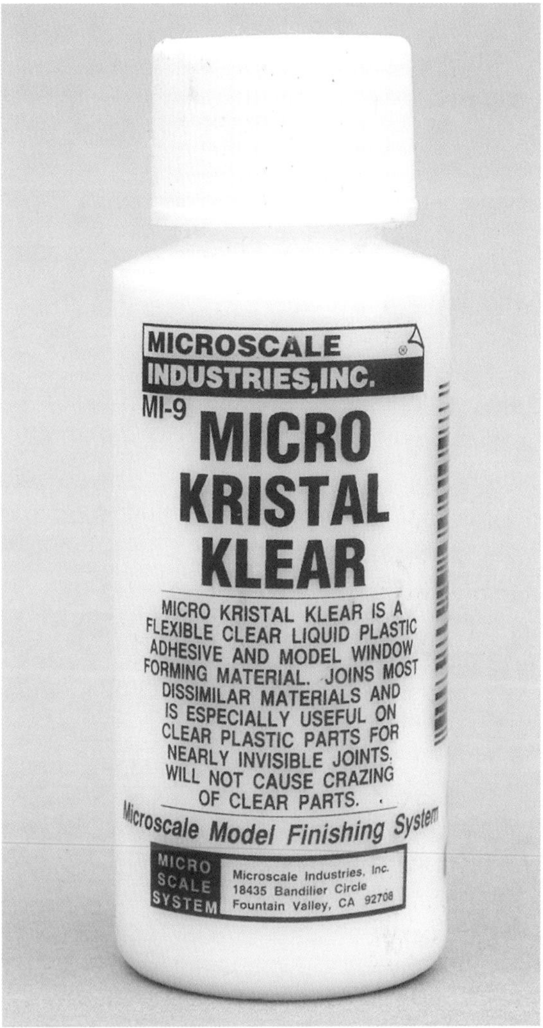

A good quality PVA has many uses and is strong enough to hold small etched parts even when thinned with water.

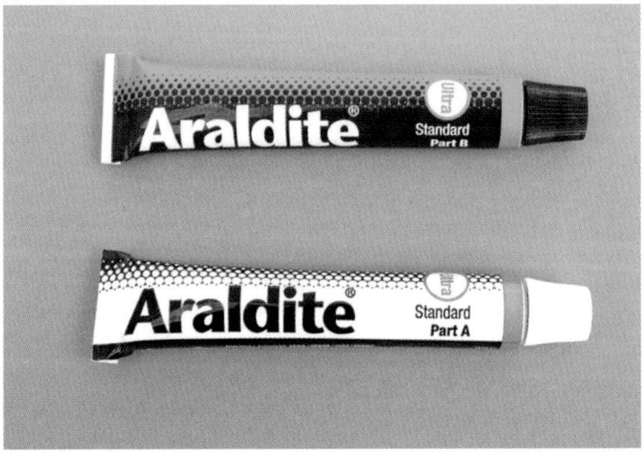

Epoxy is used infrequently as it is rather messy and smells strongly; it is best reserved for when time is needed to position the part.

When applying adhesive, most of the time it is too risky to use it straight from the bottle on to the parts, as it is very easy to apply too much and end up with a mess. Use an old piece of scrap plastic, or cover an old paint palette with foil to make a reusable glue tray. Squeeze a drop of adhesive on to your preferred glue tray, and apply it to the parts using a cocktail stick: this will give far greater control, as it is much easier to add a little more if necessary than to remove an excess.

SPECIALIST TOOLS

Most of us will have, somewhere in the house, a variety of gadgets bought on a whim, which just sit gathering dust after the first couple of uses, assuming they even make it out of the box. So, too, the modeller's box seems to attract tools that at the time seemed perfect for the task, but turn out to be no more than an expensive impulse. On the other hand, although we all make the occasional wasteful purchase, some tools that come under the 'specialist' category can turn out to be good value in the long run. 'Specialist' in this case really means a tool that is designed to do a particular job, and will do it better than the general tools mentioned in the previous section. Everyone will have their own favourites, but for me, the following have proved particularly useful.

A razor saw This is a very useful tool for cutting away apertures, removing large casting blocks, safely taking parts off thick sprues, and any similar task. The Czech manufacturer Libor Kopeček makes an excellent saw that has a well-made wooden handle, and two types of toothed blade. These blades are very thin but strong and are excellent for any of the tasks mentioned earlier. There is also the option of using two blades with the included spacing bars to give two parallel cuts. It can be a difficult tool to find, although a good way to locate quality tools is to visit the huge IPMS Scale Modelworld show in the UK, or similar shows elsewhere.

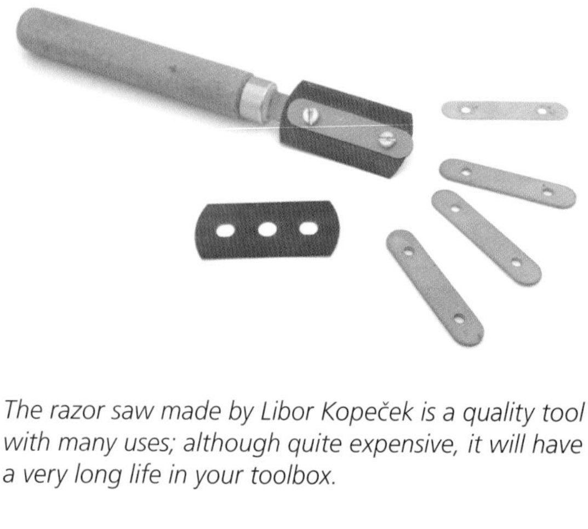

The razor saw made by Libor Kopeček is a quality tool with many uses; although quite expensive, it will have a very long life in your toolbox.

An etch folding tool As most model ship etch is very small, the need to use an etch folding tool does not arise too often. On occasion, especially when working in 1/350 scale, it can help to give clean, sharp and more accurate folds. One of the large and expensive tools isn't necessary: Trumpeter make a small etch folding tool just 6cm square, and this is ideal for the small-sized parts found in model ship etched sets.

It is unlikely that anything larger than the Trumpeter 6cm etch folding tool will be needed when working with small scales.

A micro-chisel Kits are not always perfect, and quite often it is necessary to remove moulded-on detail that isn't up to standard. Doors and ladders

The Mission Models micro-chisel has a choice of blades that are easily changed, with replacements available.

quite often fall into this category, and can easily be replaced by better etched parts once the original has been removed. For this purpose a micro-chisel is the best option: as its name implies, it is a small chisel with a very sharp blade just a few millimetres across, which can be used to cut away undesirable kit mouldings. It is best to keep these covered when not in use, to protect both the blade and your fingers. Should it get damaged, spare blades are available in different sizes.

LIGHTING AND OPTICAL AIDS

The most precious and vital tool that any modeller can have is their eyesight: it is the one tool that cannot be replaced, so it is worth investing in good lighting and visual aids to protect the eyes from undue strain and damage.

Good Lighting

Lamps made by the Daylight Company are excellent as they provide more than adequate lighting with, as the name suggests, daylight bulbs. The advantage of these is that they reduce eye strain, show a truer shade of colour, and can also provide some health benefits. It really is worth getting the best lamp you can afford; it will last you many years, and unlike that expensive kit sitting in the cupboard waiting for the right time to build it, you will get hours of use from such a lamp, both improving your modelling and helping to protect your eyesight.

Magnification

When working with very small parts, some assistance with magnification is often needed. Again, this will help prevent eye strain, although it is important to use an aid that is comfortable and does not have too high a degree of magnification, as this can have an injurious effect if you are continually moving from magnified to normal vision. For this task an Optivisor made by Donegan Optical is recommended: this is a headband with an adjustable visor, for which a range of interchangeable lenses is available. In general use something like the ×1.75 or ×2 magnification is sufficient, as this gives assistance without straining the eyes during prolonged use. These lower magnifications also give a longer focal distance, so work can be carried out at 10–12in away, rather than the much shorter and often less comfortable 4–6in distance that higher magnifications require.

In terms of visual aids it is really a matter of personal preference, as individual eyesight and

The Optivisor from Donegan Optical is a popular choice of visual aid; it is lightweight and can be used alongside spectacles.

requirements will vary greatly. If possible try out different options at your local club or at model shows, or ask friends what they use, to give yourself an idea of what will suit your particular needs.

USEFUL MATERIALS

Some essential bits and pieces don't fit into the tools category but will find frequent use or be just the thing for a difficult element of the model. First amongst these is masking tape which, as the name suggests, is needed for paint masking mostly, although it is useful for holding parts together whilst setting or for mounting parts for painting. Use model masking tape for this, Tamiya is widely accepted as the best, cheaper brands look similar but the adhesive on these is often quite gummy, especially if left on for more than a few hours or in warm temperatures. Also useful is micro-tape made by Aizu in thicknesses of less than 1mm, which is excellent for masking fine lines.

For holding parts for painting or whilst setting, wooden craft sticks along with Blu Tack is a good combination, while masking tape doubled over can be used for very small parts if needed, such as small anti-aircraft guns, as the Blu Tack will creep over the edge where it is attached and mask the part from painting. Double-sided tape can also be used, but be careful not to leave parts attached to this too long as it can get very sticky and leave residue on the parts.

There are a number of commercially available products that can be used to improve your model. Evergreen make a wide range of plastic rod, sheet and strip in different sizes and thickness; these are very useful for replacing overscale barrels, supports and bulwarks. Even finer are the brass and nickel silver rods from Albion Alloys, which can be found as small as 0.1mm; this company also makes some very nice tubing in small diameters. Brass rod makes an excellent replacement for masts when rigging is required. Solder can be used to create vents, pipes and similar, as it is easy to bend and will hold its shape.

Sheet materials that are useful include plastics, brass, copper, aluminium or any metal that can be easily cut and shaped. One of the most useful, not to mention cheap ways of making sheet material is to use paper infused with CA glue. Use a decent quality of paper and spread a few small drops of CA over the surface – only a small area will be needed. This will dry quickly and leave a hard but flexible sheet that can easily be cut, will hold its shape, and, as it is not as springy as metal, will be easier to glue into place. If the sides are a little rough, rub them over with some wet-and-dry paper.

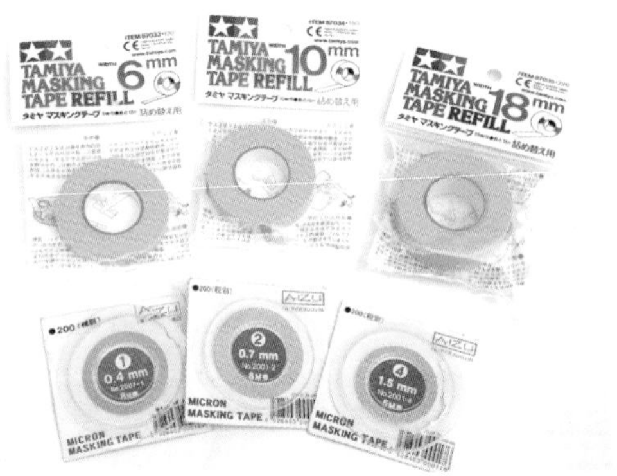

Tamiya and Aizu tapes are good quality and don't leave any residue behind; it is best to reduce tack by pressing on a clean surface before use.

Plastic rod and strip from Evergreen has many uses, and also the advantage of being consistent in size; brass rod is used when a more rigid part is required.

Chapter Three

First Steps: Building a Plastic Kit Out of the Box

What is a good starting kit for a beginner in ship modelling? This is a question commonly asked and the response is generally in two parts. First, pick some subjects that interest you; since ship models can take longer to build than other types of kit, there is much less chance of it being put aside if the subject is one that the modeller wants to see completed. The second part is to find a subject that does have at least a reasonably good kit available; nothing is more likely to be off-putting than badly fitting parts lacking detail. Those ancient Airfix and Revell kits that you built as a child might not be the best route to getting back into the hobby.

GETTING STARTED

Modern subjects are a good choice to learn the basics of building a kit out of the box; their clean lines, to reduce radar signature, mean there is generally little in the way of 'clutter' that can be found on ships from earlier periods. For our first build the kit will be the Dragon 1/700 model of the Type 45 destroyer HMS *Daring*. This is a reasonably large model in 1/700 without too many parts, although it does include some etched brass, which is an increasingly common feature of plastic kits.

Cleaning the Parts

The first important step when building any kit, plastic or resin, is to clean the parts in a bowl of warm water with a drop of washing-up liquid added. Any kit will have a greasy substance called 'mould release' still clinging to it – this is, as the name suggests, to allow the parts to come away from the mould cleanly during production. In particular, removing this will help during the painting stages, as otherwise the paint can have trouble adhering to the surface of the model. Use an old toothbrush to scrub the parts gently to make sure all the mould release is removed.

Making a Working Base

Next we will need a working base so that the model is not handled too much during construction. This will help prevent damage and also reduce contact with fingers, which will lead to dirt and grease being left on the model. A piece of pine or similar softwood makes a good base; make sure it is wider than the beam of the model and a little longer than the hull length to give some room to hold it.

Mark two or three holes in the base of the hull and drill these out partly into the wooden base. Then remove the hull and drill through the base: screws will be used to attach the model to the base, so choose a suitable diameter of drill

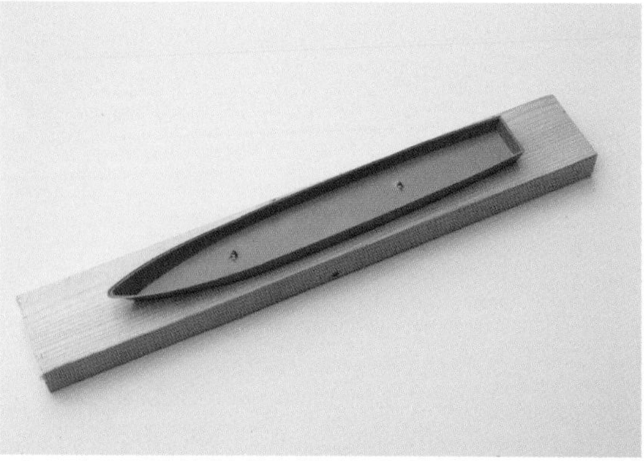

The hull of the model attached to a working base, in this case a piece of softwood 4 × 2cm, a few centimetres longer than the hull to allow for grip.

bit. The screws used should be long enough to go through the base and hold the ship, but not too long that they will interfere with any part of the model. Although the working base can be removed when the model is completed, the holes in the hull bottom can be used to fix it to the final base if required.

Finish the attachment to the working base by screwing through the wood back into the model, taking care not to do this too quickly to avoid damage to the model. Also be careful not to over-tighten the screws, as this can cause distortion of the hull, which will settle back into its original shape when the model is removed, inevitably leading to parts already fitted being displaced.

Now you have your starting point to be able to work around the model easily.

PLANNING AND PREPARATION

One of the main differences between building ships and other types of model is the greater need for planning. Ships are in general far more complex in form; this makes for a more visually interesting model, but it also means that putting it together requires more thought. There is no one hard and fast procedure for doing this; it very much depends on the subject and how the kit is constructed, so to some extent the process will vary with each individual model.

The steps of building the model need to be planned around the painting sequence, as some areas will inevitably be difficult to reach without causing damage to parts already in place, or spoiling previous paintwork. Some modellers are able to more or less complete construction of a model before painting, and I find that extremely impressive. Others tend to work on sub-assemblies, constructing superstructure elements separately and painting these before a final assembly. Finding a style that suits is a matter of personal taste to a large extent; the following chapters will show how the subject of the model can dictate how it is built and painted.

There is no such thing as a perfect kit: all kits will include compromises of accuracy and detail resulting from the production process and the expected end price to the customer. From that perspective every kit can be seen as a starting point along the route towards producing the final model. Of course, some provide more of a head start on the journey towards the finishing line than others, but where you want that line to be is very much your own choice. Any model can be built either out of the box or with added detail, according to the modeller's wishes.

Before You Start

Before starting the model it pays to look at reference books or have a quick search on the internet for photos and information about the subject. For those keen to have the most accurate model possible, there are often sets of plans available to check dimensions and the accuracy of the kit. Researching a model can in itself be a fascinating and rewarding part of the hobby – it goes without saying that there is a huge library of books on naval and mercantile subjects available. These can be expensive, however, so make use of your local library and the inter-library loan system if you need a particular reference. Before starting the model, take some time to gather reference material as it will help you understand the subject better, and may indicate some areas of detail on the kit that you wish to improve.

Take a look through the kit parts and see if any are not up to standard, and consider if you want to replace them from aftermarket items. Similarly, if you wish to add etched detail, look for options for enhancement: in both cases it is best to have everything that you will need to hand before you start to build the model.

Clear your modelling area before starting work, and place the tools you will need to use near to hand. Remove any clutter from the area: you will be sure to have some parts that launch themselves away from the sprue, and it makes them much easier to find on a clear bench. If you don't have a dedicated workbench, a large tray makes a very useful substitute. Find a suitable-sized cover for your model, and for any parts that have been assembled and set aside. This will both prevent damage and keep dust off the model during the building process.

With all this in place, we are ready to start.

BUILDING THE DRAGON MODEL OF HMS *DARING*

This model of the Type 45 destroyer HMS *Daring* is a relatively straightforward kit. The fit of parts is quite good, and as a modern subject, it is quite a clean and uncluttered ship because of the requirements of reducing radar signature. This makes it a good first kit, because even though it includes a small etched brass fret, this is simple to use and a good way to get over any fears of using this medium.

As shown earlier, the first task is to attach the model to the working base. Once this has been done, a quick look through the instructions indicates that the build sequence suggested is not in fact a very sensible one. By far the easiest and best way to begin any model is to put in place the deck and largest superstructures first. Should these need filling, the action of sanding will guarantee to result in any small parts being knocked off, damaged or lost. Don't be afraid to ignore the kit instructions if you feel that you have a better method.

Fitting the Deck

The deck is therefore the first part to be assembled. When removing parts from the sprue use your cutters to cut away at the attachment point a few millimetres from the part; this prevents any damage to the part around this area. Then use your scalpel to cut back on the sprue attachment, and clean up the part with a sanding stick or similar.

A superstructure part removed from the sprue with the attachment still in place; it is safer to clean up the part away from the sprue as damage is less likely.

The same part cleaned up; once it is flush to the surface, run the sanding stick lightly around the edge of the whole part to remove any rough edges.

Test fit the main parts by putting them into place and seeing if there are any gaps or areas of poor fit. If you have to work on a part a little to get it to fit, it is better to do that than it is to glue it in place and then have to reach for the filler later. It is unlikely that you will get as good a result from using large amounts of filler on a badly fitted part than you will if, with a little time and effort, you can get it to fit as well as you can. In this case, although the deck fits very well and needs just a little work on the whole, the bow is slightly too long to fit in the hull recess, and the tip is left protruding. Some work with the sanding stick is not enough to prevent this, so excess plastic has to be scraped away with the flat of the scalpel blade to reduce the thickness of the part.

Once this is done, the fit is much better and the part can then be glued into place using some liquid poly cement run around the groove on the top of the hull. Should any cement be forced up around the deck edge as the part is placed, don't be tempted to try and remove this straightaway as it will damage the surrounding area. Leave it to dry, then sand away any excess before filling.

Before applying filler, scrape the edge of the scalpel blade around the deck edge to reduce any lip. Be careful not to press too hard: the idea is to remove any raised area so less filler will be required. A few small gaps around the deck edge can then be filled; in this case Humbrol filler is used as it dries quickly and works well for very small gaps on plastic kits. Anything flat with a little flexibility can be used as a tool to apply the filler, as it will help work it into the gap. Leave the filler to dry for half an hour or so, then sand it down, at first with a medium-grade sanding stick or wet-and-dry paper (800 grade is fine), then use a fine-grade stick to polish up any marks, to leave a smooth finish.

With the deck in place, test fitting shows a small misalignment between the front of the

Any bubbling up of cement around joins should be left for an hour to dry before sanding away. Remove the rest of the main parts from the sprue while you are waiting.

Poor fit can be corrected with a little work; the part is slightly too long so needs to be cut back and thinned to make a better fit.

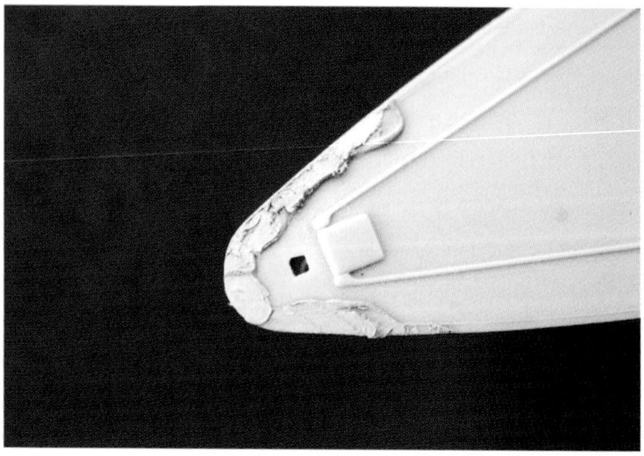

Filler applied to the gap around the bow-deck area; it doesn't matter that it looks rough at this stage as it will sand to a smooth finish.

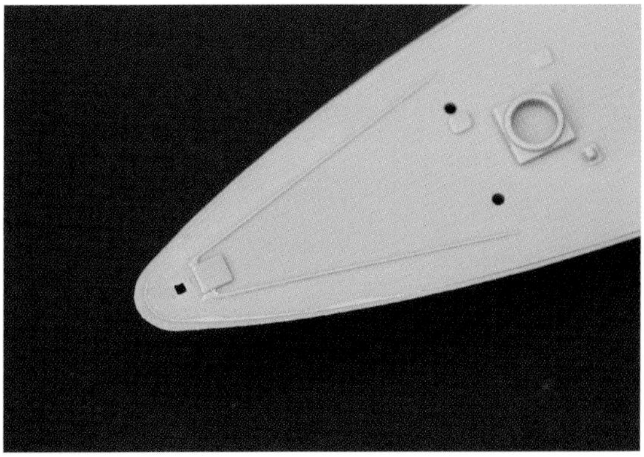

Finished bow sanding: the join should be invisible, but the filler can shrink so if necessary repeat the process.

When using plastic card or similar as a filler it is easier to cut larger and trim to size.

superstructure and the deck part, forming a small cutout. This will leave a small but unsightly gap; on a clean ship such as HMS *Daring* this needs to be fixed. An easy way to do this is to use a small piece of plastic card – in this case 10-thou card is thick enough – cut to a larger size than the area to be filled. Glue it in place with Mek Pak as this will dry quickly, then leave it to go completely dry and harden. Now with a fresh scalpel blade, trim down the insert to the correct size, and the gap is easily and accurately filled.

Small gaps where parts do not fit perfectly are common; it is possible to fill these cleanly with a little effort.

Adding the Main Superstructure Parts

Next the main superstructure parts are added. As there is a clean angle between the edge of the hull and the superstructure, this needs to be made as sharp as possible. Application of filler is followed first by tidying up with sanding sticks, then using progressively finer grades of polishing pad to result in a smooth and polished finish.

One thing to consider when building very small scales is that the tolerance for any blemishes on the model has to be much less. Consider that in 1/700 scale the size of a figure would be around 5mm, then take a look at your model with that in

Polishing the hull with progressively finer grades of wet-and-dry paper or polishing pads will give a smooth surface for painting.

1. Small gaps in hard-to-reach places can be filled by following a few steps, as it will be difficult to get a clean join just using filler.

2. As the gap is narrow, paper infused with superglue is pushed in with the scalpel tip to act as an initial filler.

3. Using a fresh scalpel, trim the paper to give a clean and sharp edge.

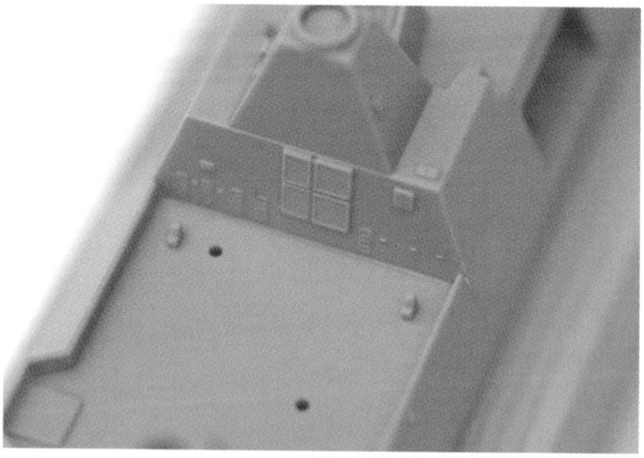

4. The repair is filled with Mr Surfacer, which is cleaned off with a cotton bud dipped in Mr Color Thinner to give a neat finish.

mind and think whether what you have is good enough. A friend said to me that he thought the sign of a good modeller was what they would say on spotting an error on a model, whether 'it's good enough' or 'I'll put it right'. It's a valuable thought to have in mind in any type of modelling.

The two superstructure parts fit well together, but there is a slight gap between the main deck and the hangar – only small, but large enough for a 1/700 crew member to fall through. This would be tricky to fill with thicker filler, and Mr Surfacer needs a little help to be able to cover the gap. The sequence for filling difficult-to-reach gaps such as this is shown in the photos.

Continuing with construction, any small gaps are filled and care is taken to smooth the joins in between the main parts. Any mould seams along the parts are removed by carefully scraping with the edge of the scalpel blade. Modern ships are very angular, so it is important that there are no offset edges or rounded angles.

Once the main parts have all been assembled, work moves on to the smaller parts; it is then time to consider how the model will be painted, and if adding any of these small parts will make this task more difficult. Some of these parts are set aside still attached to a small section of sprue, since very

Scraping away a mould seam with the flat blade of the scalpel is less likely to cause damage to the part than filing, which can easily be overdone.

Small parts are grouped by the colour they will be painted; very small parts can be left attached to a section of sprue.

small parts are difficult to mount for painting. A wooden craft stick is very useful for holding these parts ready for painting, especially as they can be grouped according to the colour they are to be painted, if needs be.

At this point it became obvious that there was a mistake in the kit instructions, and the parts used to close the apertures for the accommodation ladders should in fact be placed from the inside, not the outside as shown. Some thick (60-thou) plastic card plugs the gap nicely, and this is then filled and sanded, as photos of the ship show that it is very hard to see this area. If you are in any doubt should an error like this occur, take a look at your reference photos for guidance.

The Small Photoetched Fret

With all the main superstructure parts assembled and small parts set aside for painting separately, it is time to move to the small photoetched fret. A small fret is often included in modern plastic kits to provide for better detailed parts most benefiting from it, including items such as cranes and catapults. For the HMS *Daring* kit the etched parts are for the hangar and boat-deck doors, the foremast aerials, accommodation ladders and flight-deck netting. It is a small fret and a good opportunity to make a start with photoetch.

As with the plastic parts, the first step is to clean off any residue; again this is done with hot water and a small drop of washing-up liquid – the water can be a little hotter than for plastic, as the parts are much less likely to distort. Leave them in the hot-water bath for a few minutes, rinse under cold water and leave to air dry until needed. Do not be tempted to try and dry them with kitchen roll or similar, as fibres will become attached to the etch. Cleaning etch in this way will help with the adhesion of both glue and paint. Use tweezers for placing etch if possible, or at least try to hold larger parts by the edge and handle as little as you can.

Photoetched parts are normally made from very thin brass: 0.1mm is standard, although thicker sheet is used. For 1/350 scale kits especially, when there are large components, nickel silver or stainless steel may be used as this gives greater strength – although as a result it is harder to cut and is less forgiving to any folding errors. Some modellers like to paint the etch with a primer before starting work; this is a personal choice, but it can lead to problems if the primer does not adhere properly to the metal, as it can come away once glued. Only cut out the parts when you need them, as they can be easily lost or damaged.

Cutting Photoetched Parts

The best way to cut photoetch is on a hard surface – a piece of thick glass or offcut ceramic tile is ideal. Cutting etch on the cutting mat will lead to it being bent into the mat and damaged as a result. A hard surface is needed so that it will retain its original shape until it needs to be folded. Use the rounded no. 10 scalpel blade to cut the etch with a rocking motion: this will help to prevent damage and it will also be less likely for parts to fly off the fret and get lost. As with the plastic parts, leave a small stub, as this is easier to trim with sharp scissors; then finish off with a few swipes of the sanding stick, taking care once more not to bend the part.

An offcut of a tile or hardened glass makes an ideal base for cutting etched brass parts, and will cost nothing.

Trim the stub off the part with small scissors to give a clean edge; trimming the stub in this way is easier than trying to cut it off cleanly whilst on the fret.

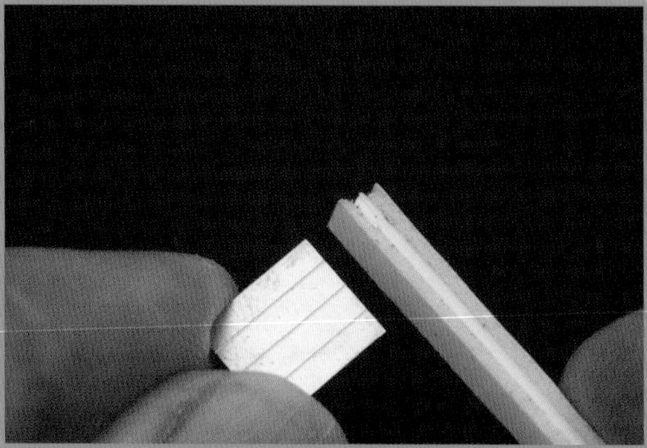

Finish off the part by gently sanding the stub to remove any burrs that may have gone unnoticed.

Simple etched parts such as the hangar doors and boat screens found in this kit can be fixed in place with CA glue or PVA. The latter gives more time to correct alignment, so is preferable in this case. Replacement brass parts for the antenna for the foremast are also provided, but sometimes the plastic parts are better than the brass ones, so they were not used. It is always worth making your own decision as to whether to use etched brass replacement parts – they are not always necessarily the best option.

Flight-deck netting is also included as a brass part; this was fixed in place with PVA – a small strip of masking tape can be used to hold the part in place while this sets. With the model assembled and small parts mounted for painting separately, we can move on to thinking about the best sequence of painting.

PAINTING BASICS

Model painting is one of the most complex areas of the hobby and deserves a separate chapter of its own, which indeed is the case for this book. We will discuss topics such as choice of paint, methods of application and weathering in much greater detail later. Some simple principles are applied to all models, however, and it is best to get into good habits at an early stage.

Looking at the HMS *Daring* model, once assembly has been finished there will be particles of dust that have collected on the model from sanding and the general surroundings. Model aircraft builders often wash their models to remove the grease from fingerprints to improve paint adhesion, but because in this case a wooden base has been used to reduce handling, this won't be necessary. Use a large soft brush to remove any dust deposits, or if you have one, an airbrush: this will help in achieving a smooth paint finish.

The Primer Coat

Once this is done, the first step is a primer coat, as this will help not only to give the paint better

The primed model is left to dry for a couple of hours; primers are formulated to bond and seal the surface, and result in a much better finish.

adhesion, but it is also very useful as a means to spot any areas of sanding or joins that have not been properly finished. With the HMS *Daring* model an aerosol plastic primer available from the car-part retailer Halfords was used, as this gives a good enough coat of primer that is quick and easy to apply. A few quick sprays over the model at a distance of around 20–30cm is sufficient to give an overall coat of primer, though be careful not to flood the model as the paint is quite thick and detail can be lost if the coat is too heavy. This is left to dry before inspecting for any errors: these can then be corrected with a little more filler or application of the sanding stick before painting.

Now comes the dilemma true of every ship model: is it easier to paint the deck first, or the hull and superstructure? In general, the more complicated the superstructure, the harder it will be to paint the deck. With models such as this it is better to paint the deck first, then mask this work before moving on. The exception to this would be aircraft carriers, where the deck can very easily be masked while the hull is much more difficult.

Another basis for making the decision is whether you are hand brushing, or using an airbrush, since this can again dictate the best order. If the model has a wooden deck and this is to be hand painted, it is much better to do this first. If there is a steel deck and one colour, this is much simpler and it is often easier to paint the deck second and use a little masking around the superstructure. As a general principle, if in doubt paint the deck first, as this will usually be the easiest option.

Preparing to Paint

As a modern ship, the Type 45 destroyer HMS *Daring* has a simple superstructure that is blocky and angular – some might even call it a little unattractive. This does mean, though, that the deck areas are regular shapes, which makes for easier painting since it is free of the clutter of hatches, cable reels and bollards found on earlier vessels. For this reason, the procedure this time will be to paint the base colour overall first, then paint the deck by hand. The Type 45s have a high boot topping (the black line denoting the usual waterline), but this will be difficult to mask off as it will be a narrow band at the bottom of the hull, so it is left until last.

First though, some black panels on the superstructure behind the masts are painted black as these will be easy to mask. Once dried, the panels are masked; it is easier to cut the masking tape into small strips to outline the masked area, then fill in the remainder, than to try and cut a mask to the exact size. Should the masking tape be too tacky, rub it down on to a clean cutting mat and lift it off a few times: this will reduce the tackiness and make it less likely to lift the paint when it is time to remove it. Try not to leave masking tape on the model for too long, as after a few days in place it can start to adhere to the paint, greatly increasing the risk of it lifting the paint off.

Painting the Base Colour

With masking complete, painting the base colour is carried out with an airbrush and using an oil-based enamel paint, Sovereign Hobbies Light Weatherwork Grey. The whole of the model is painted so as to ensure no areas are missed and to give a basis for the deck painting. Two light coats are sufficient to give a good overall base colour; a few hours drying in a warm room is enough to harden off the paint before the second coat is applied. This is then left at least overnight to ensure it is completely dry before starting with deck painting.

Deck Painting

Sovereign Hobbies paint is again used for the deck, this time Royal Navy Dark Deck Grey, which is brush painted. The areas of deck around the superstructures are first outlined with a medium-sized brush before filling in the remainder. Don't try and do all this at once: again, better results will be achieved by applying several thin coats rather than one thick one. Thin the paint from

Masking is best carried out by using small strips of tape to mark out the edges of the area to be covered, then filling in the centre.

When the base colour is painted with an airbrush, it is easier to paint the entire model. Brush painting can be more selective.

the pot with a little thinner and gradually work around the model. There will inevitably be areas to touch up, so these can be returned to once the deck has completely dried. If paint has been applied a little thickly in parts, lightly rub over these patches with a fine sanding pad or similar before the final coat.

Once painting is complete the masking tape is carefully removed and any overspray touched up with a small brush. In order to give a better surface for the addition of decals, and a smooth finish that will help with weathering, a couple of coats of gloss varnish are sprayed over the whole of the model. If you try to cover only the areas where decals are needed, this can produce a patchy effect.

DECALS

Not all models will need decals, but it is important to know how to use them properly, because if poorly applied they can spoil the previous work. A gloss surface is the easiest way to prevent the decal silvering and causing the clear backing to show. This is caused by air being trapped between the decal and the model surface. Matt paints leave a rougher surface than gloss and are therefore more likely to cause silvering.

Where decals are needed it is safer to use a gloss varnish first; in any case this will seal in the previous layers of paint. Cut out each decal so they can be used separately, and place each one into a container of warm water until it starts to loosen from the backing. Lift the decal out of the water and let any excess drain off; if necessary touch

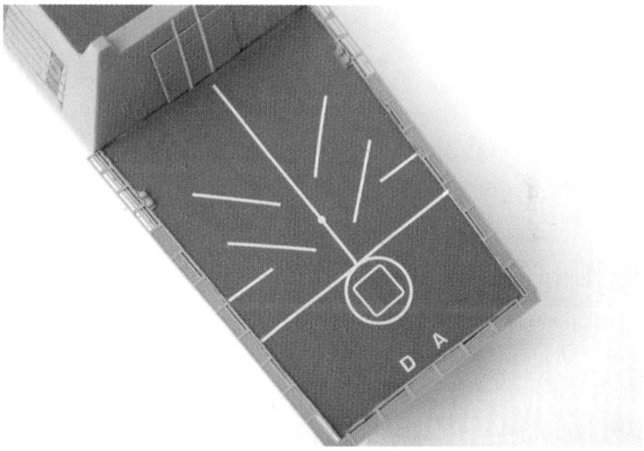

With deck painting finished the flight-deck decals are placed after first airbrushing on a couple of gloss layers.

The bridge is a prominent feature of many modern ships in particular; decal strip gives a very clean and sharp choice for the windows.

the corner to a piece of kitchen towel to help with this. Place on to the model and position into place gently with a cocktail stick. To finish, use a cotton bud to seal the decal carefully on to the surface, removing any final dampness at the same time.

Once decals have been added, small details are picked out, such as radar domes, and anything else requiring a different colour that will help to break up the overall monotone light grey of the hull and superstructure. Black decal strip cut to size is used for the bridge windows, as this gives a sharper and cleaner edge than painting can achieve. Some use of Lifecolor grey liner is applied to show wear and tear, but no weathering. The model is then completed with a few coats of Alclad light sheen varnish; this produces a dulled down but not completely flat matt finish, which is more suitable for ships.

We will take a more in-depth look at painting techniques and materials in their own chapter later in the book, since this is such a major part of any model making.

FINISHING OFF

To finish off, HMS *Daring* is placed on to a seabase from Coastal Kits. These are photographic reproductions of water with a wave effect on a stiff foamboard backing, and make for a very effective and extremely simple display. Although the board is flat, it could be built up to create a bow wave to enhance the effect; but for a quick and easy way to improve the display of your models, these are excellent.

As an out-of-the-box build there are some areas of the model that could have been bettered. In the next chapter we will see how a basic kit can be brought up to a much higher level by working to improve some weak areas, and will consider the type of aftermarket parts currently available that can help with this.

The finished model set on a base from Coastal Kits, from a typical plastic kit built out of the box; it is a very fine-looking model.

Chapter Four

Taking it Further: Improving a Plastic Kit

All of us when we start building models tend to assume that the manufacturer has got it right, and the kit will be accurate with correct details. As subject knowledge and skills improve, it becomes obvious that this is, if anything, very rarely the case. Most kits have some degree of inaccuracy, and the challenge – and indeed a great part of the interest and fun of building ship models – is to carry out research to determine any changes that are required, and to seek to produce a more accurate model.

The first step is to gather some reference material. There is a huge amount of information available on the internet, including some highly detailed plans that are free to download. However, for accuracy and quality of information it is still difficult to better the printed word, and some superb material is available – any reference work by Raven, Burt or Friedman, for example, will be worth having. Check the kit parts against the plans to see where any alterations may be needed, and look at reference photos of the period you wish to show in your model. Doing this will help you to see if any changes are needed; for example weapons and, for later ships, radar fits change and upgrade continually, so may need to be altered.

By getting into the habit of looking at a kit critically and checking for errors, you will learn to understand better how ships work, and will produce more accurate and satisfying models as a result. A good approach is to consider any kit merely as a starting point, and from this you will add your own individual stamp in terms of detailing and improvement.

IMPROVING THE BASIC KIT OF USS *WASP*

Quite often when a particular subject appeals the choice of kit is quite limited, so it is necessary to take whatever is on offer and find ways in which to improve it. The 1/700 kit of the US Navy aircraft carrier USS *Wasp* CV-7 by Aoshima is, by modern standards, a fairly average kit. Details are reasonable but the small parts are poor and would be better replaced. In some areas moulding is very

Replacing overscale areas such as these shields will greatly improve the final look of the model.

heavy and out of scale, and bulwarks and shields around the deck levels and anti-aircraft weapons in particular need some attention. Similarly the aircraft are either not particularly well done, are incorrect, or will need improving.

USS *Wasp* was a one-off ship designed to take advantage of tonnage allowed to the USA for aircraft carrier construction under the Washington Naval Treaty. She was built with very limited armour and no protection against torpedoes, as this would have taken her over the allowable tonnage. Unsurprisingly she had a short career, although an eventful one, the most significant operation involving two missions to the Mediterranean carrying British fighter aircraft for the defence of Malta. To undertake this, she docked at Scapa Flow in the Shetland Islands to fly off her own aircraft in preparation for embarking RAF Spitfires. This unusual action will be the subject of the model, showing *Wasp* approaching the harbour in preparation for landing her own aircraft, which will be readying on deck.

Helpfully, a set of plans for *Wasp* is available for download, and even though these show the ship as built, any differences to the particular time period being modelled can be identified with reference to photographs. The first step is to look over the kit whilst consulting the plans to determine where improvements might be made, and if necessary, where replacement parts might be needed. Aoshima produce a photoetched set for the kit, which will be used: this provides railings, flight deck, aircraft, radars and other small details, all of which will help to improve some of the shortcomings of the kit. In this case a wooden replacement will be used for the flight deck; this also comes with some etched brass details to replace those that will have to be removed to allow the deck to be fitted.

With the combination of the kit, the etched set and the wooden deck, as well as some replacement small parts, planning and reference to the various sets of instructions is again important so as not to miss anything that might be difficult to add later.

IMPROVEMENTS TO THE BASIC HULL

Construction of the basic hull proceeds with first modifying those parts most obviously in need of improvement. The various platforms and splinter shields around the anti-aircraft weapons are an obvious target, as it is common for injection plastic kits to have shields that are both too thick and too low in profile, resembling a garden hedge more than the thin metal they actually are. This is due to the limitations of the injection-moulding process.

Correcting the Splinter Shields

These can be corrected in two ways: first, by removing the plastic and replacing it with some other suitable material such as thin plastic card, metal or even paper thickened with CA glue. All these materials have their advantages, but sheet aluminium, which can be bought cheaply from some hobby suppliers, is excellent as it can be found suitably thin, can be easily bent, and holds its shape well. This is particularly useful when difficult shapes have to be formed, such as around the gun tubs for the low-angle weapons on *Wasp*. On the whole it is better to replace the shield round the edge of the platform rather than on top of it,

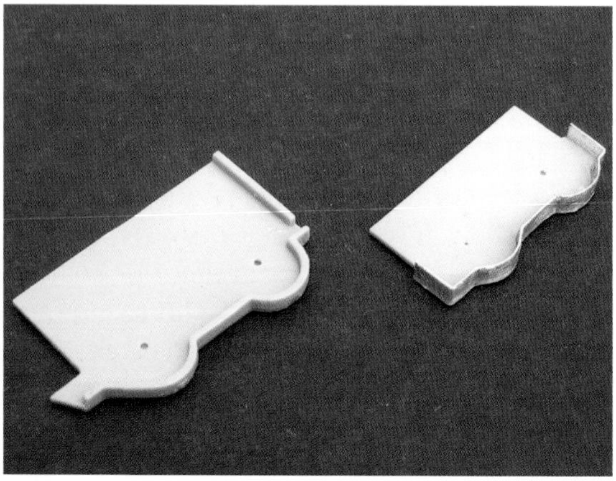

Shields that are too thick and too low can be replaced with any suitable material; here 0.1mm aluminium sheet is being used.

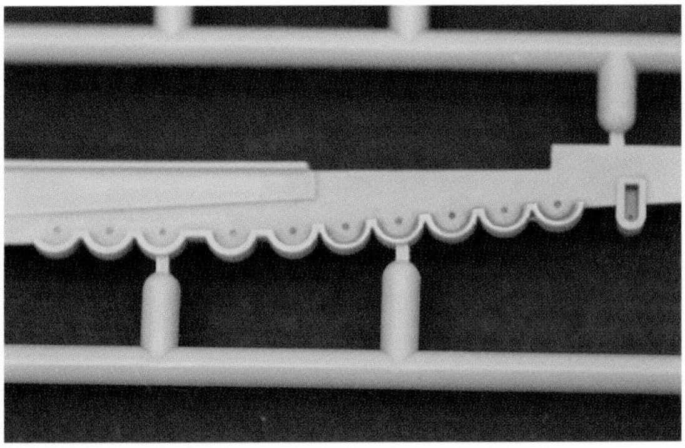

Thinning overscale shields and bulwarks is easy to do and makes a difference; those on the left are the kit part, while those on the right have been thinned down.

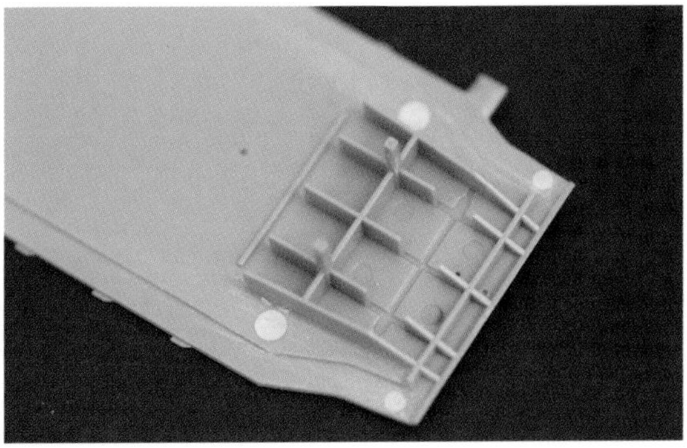

Detail under the flight deck needs to be removed to allow replacement photoetched parts to be fitted; care needs to be taken not to gouge out too much of the plastic.

as this results in both a neater edge and a larger area for the glue to grab on to. It is difficult to get enough adhesive to hold on the very thin edge of the metal to keep the part in place.

In some cases replacement of the shields is too difficult, especially where repeated shapes would need to be identical or the result will not look right. This is the case for the row of light anti-aircraft weapons found on platforms along the deck edge. Here the best solution is to scrape away the inside of the shield with a sharp scalpel so that the width of the plastic is reduced. Usually it won't be possible to reduce the full thickness of the plastic and a triangle cross-section will result, with the top much thinner than the bottom. This is, in fact, perfectly adequate, as only the top edge of the shield will in any case be noticeable.

Replacing Moulded Plastic Parts

Working around the hull and flight deck, some of the moulded plastic parts have etched brass replacements, and these require the original to be removed. The supports under the forward flight deck need to replaced, and this has to be done cleanly so that the etched brass will fit properly. To remove parts such as this, first reduce them with a saw or scalpel so that only a couple of millimetres are left; this can then be shaved and filed away to leave a smooth surface, with filler added where there may have been some over-enthusiastic cutting.

Once this has been removed there will, of course, be no guide marks remaining to show where the replacement parts need to be positioned. In this case the deck is dry fitted, and the leading edge of the superstructure marked off with the scalpel so that once removed, a clear line will indicate where the brass parts will need to be placed so they butt up against the adjacent superstructure.

The Lifts

A little visual interest can be added to the carrier deck by showing the lifts at something other than

Detailing does not always have to be complicated: a simple idea such as changing the height of the hangar lift helps to make a difference.

the fully raised or fully lowered position. This is simply done by cutting some square-section plastic rod into small lengths and gluing these on to the lift floor, so that it can be shown partly raised.

Inclined Ladders

This kit features a number of the old-style 'Aztec steps', which are intended to replicate inclined ladders; the term relates to the solid stone steps found on ancient buildings. Although in this case not completely blocked in, they still need to be removed to allow the replacement etched parts to be fitted.

Inclined ladders are one of the simplest and most common etched brass parts, but even so they are commonly used incorrectly. Folding the side handrails is a simple task, but placing the ladders at the correct angle is where many make an error. Once folded, the handrails will give an angled stanchion at the top of the ladder, and this should be at 90 degrees to the deck, so that it lines up with the adjacent railings. It is easier to place the ladder first, then the railing, but if possible try to avoid any small gaps between where the ladder will be, and where the railing will have to join. It is paying attention to such small areas of detail that will help to improve the overall quality of your finished model.

Improving the Fit of Parts

In places the fit of parts is less than perfect, and attention must be given to these areas before progressing. This can create an opportunity for a better result than merely filling and sanding the join. As the aft end of the superstructure has a solid splinter shield around it, a piece of aluminium sheet is used to cap the untidy end; extended upwards it also forms the shield. The edges of the sheet help to give a crisp edge to the superstructure, as can be seen on the completed model.

An untidy join may be better covered with a section of thin brass or aluminium sheet, especially where topped by a splinter shield.

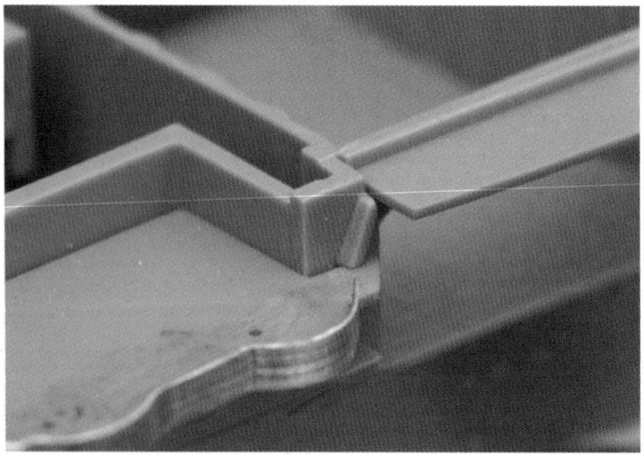

'Aztec steps' were common on older kits to represent inclined ladders. They are so called after the stone steps found on Aztec temples.

A clean and sharp finish on the completed model shows how the splinter shield has been formed from the capped end of the superstructure.

GOING FURTHER WITH PHOTOETCH

Photoetched parts can be used to augment or completely replace kit components, as well as offering entirely new parts altogether. Light anti-aircraft weapons are a common area to look to improve the level of detail, and there are many options to do so. Plastic parts generally have barrels and shields that are much too thick, and these are better suited to etched brass. Some etched sets can be highly detailed, but can also be difficult to construct, given the size.

Building Small Parts

When a number of weapons are needed, such as the 20mm Oerlikon gun found in large numbers on late World War II warships, this can be a time-consuming element of the model. Building large numbers of small and fiddly parts can be either a curse or a blessing: for some, the Zen-like process of repeatedly making something small and intricate helps in the important relaxation element of modelling; others may look for something a little quicker.

A good compromise for these very common small weapons, as in the build of USS *Wasp*, is to use a quality plastic item, in this case by Flyhawk, with etched brass gun shields to give a finer level of detail than is possible with just plastic. Similarly, etched brass shields and rails can be added to other commonly used light AA weapons to give an extra degree of detail.

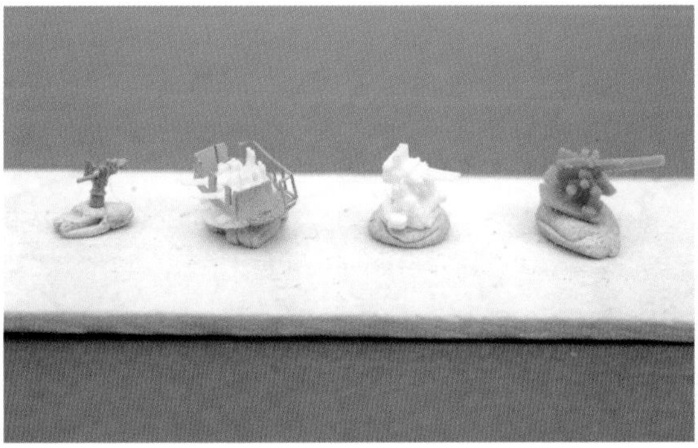

Anti-aircraft guns including Flyhawk 20mm with etched brass shields, Niko quad 40mm and 1.1in and 3D Modelparts 5in guns.

After painstaking work building small parts, it is good practice to mount them on a wooden craft stick with Blu Tack or double-sided tape. This prevents the parts from getting lost or damaged, and means they are also ready for painting. Store the mounted parts in a dust-proof box until they are needed. Craft shops sell A4-sized, lidded plastic boxes for storage, and these are cheap and very handy for this purpose.

Most ships prior to the very modern age would have complicated, open structures that are best represented in small scales by photoetched parts. Commonly these will include cranes, aircraft catapults, radar arrays, lattice masts and support structures.

Working with Etched Parts

Learning to work cleanly and accurately with etched parts is an essential skill, which takes only a little practice to master. There are a lot of etched bending tools available, but most of these are intended for larger-scale aircraft and armour models; only the smallest size of these will see any regular use in smaller scales. Instead, most etch work can be accomplished with the use of tweezers, a scalpel or single-edged razor blades and a straight-edge.

Working as before on a hard surface such as thick glass or tile, remove the part to be built from the etch fret and clean up any sprue tags. To fold simple shapes, bring the flat edge against the fold, place the blade underneath the part to be folded, and lift it up until it is at the desired angle. The flat edge helps to hold down the part whilst it is being folded, and it will also keep the fold clean and sharp.

If you make a mistake, flatten the part down with the flat edge and try again; be aware, though, that etched brass is very thin, and there will only be so many opportunities to get it right. For more complex and smaller shapes, tweezers are likely to be the most useful, especially when the width of the fold hinge is very small. Those with a flat,

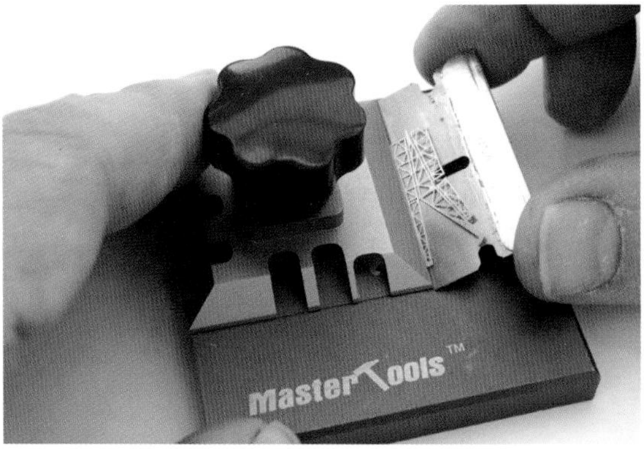

A small folding tool is very useful for keeping longer folds sharp and straight, such as this crane jib.

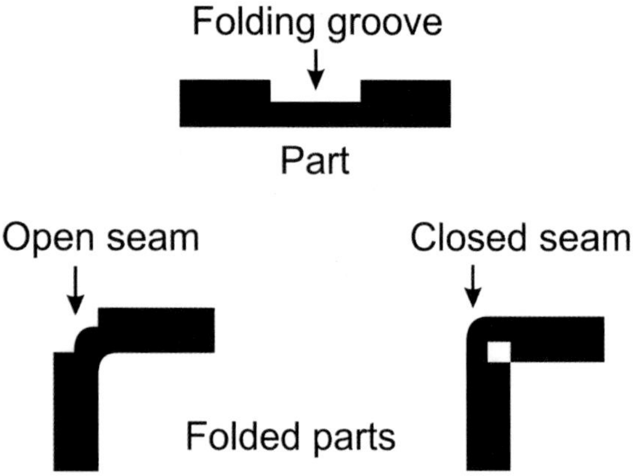

This diagram shows how photoetched parts should ideally be folded with the groove inwards so as to prevent a seam on the outside of the finished part.

rather than a pointed edge can be especially useful for folding smaller parts or when bending railing.

Parts such as lattice masts and cranes will always have one open side to be joined; however, the thin metal edges can make this difficult, as there is very little surface for any glue to hold on to. If this is a problem, a strip of plastic can be used to increase the surface area of the join by placing this inside the structure along one of the edges to be closed.

Photoetched parts that require folding will have either a short hinge of brass in between the parts, or a groove along which it is to be folded. If grooved, ideally the part will be folded so that this is along the inside of the completed assembly, otherwise there will be an open seam along the outside. However, it may not always be possible to do this if there is detail on the part, or it has to be placed in a particular position. In this case the best option is to use filler to round off the edge.

If the part cannot be folded inwards on to the groove, or it has hinges, some filler will round off the edge more satisfactorily.

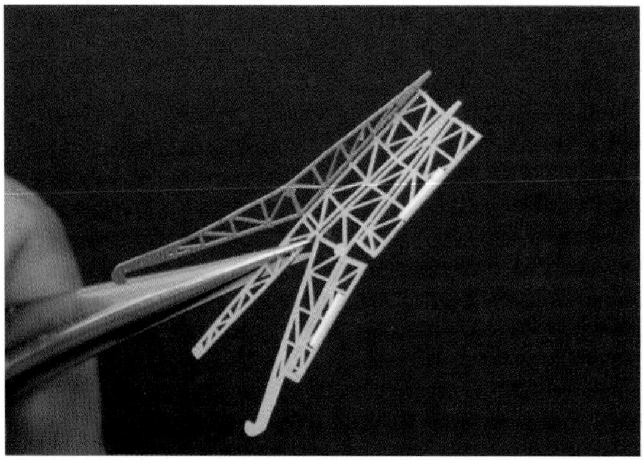

Joints in masts and cranes are strengthened by the addition of a strip of plastic; this will also help hide the seam.

Annealing Etched Brass

Digressing from the *Wasp* build briefly, there are some shapes commonly found in etched brass that need a little more work to achieve their designed appearance. Brass can be softened to allow the shape to be formed by annealing – put simply, this is the process of heating the metal until it becomes more malleable and easier to shape. This is achieved by passing the part through a candle flame for a few seconds; it will take on a bluish hue when it has been sufficiently treated. Round platforms with screens, funnel caps and similar that require anything more than a simple bend can be produced in this way. The photos below show the process of treating a searchlight platform of an HMS *London* model. As the brass becomes softer it is much easier to produce regular curves – a piece of round plastic rod can help with this.

The completed part in position with the screen curved around it; any small gaps can be filled with thinned PVA glue.

An etched brass part that combines a circular platform, and a solid rail that needs to be curved around it.

The same part treated by annealing; the brass will turn a blue colour – do not carry on heating beyond this point.

Funnel caps are usually presented as a flat piece intended to be turned into a dome shape; however, it is not possible to form this without annealing the part, as it will buckle and deform. To form the dome shape, first anneal the brass, then place it on a piece of foam offcut. Using the rounded end of a pencil or similar, push the part into the foam until the desired shape is achieved. Should there be any buckling of the rim, this can be returned to the correct shape with tweezers. This method can also be used for radar dishes requiring a similarly rounded shape.

Forming a dome-shaped funnel cap from the flat etched part; use the pencil end to create the desired shape gradually.

The completed funnel cap for HMS London*; it is attached using PVA or slow-setting CA so it can be positioned exactly.*

Improving the Superstructure

Aircraft carriers have only a small superstructure, so this needs to be given extra attention. Certain areas of a model will naturally draw the eye: weapons, the bridge and aircraft are all a particular focus of attention, so it is worth spending a little more time on these. *Wasp* had a small bridge, but it is still quite a feature; the kit part is not up to scratch here, as it is too low and does not replicate the large windows well. Detail sets do not always provide the extras required, and it is well worth keeping any etched brass left over after a model is completed, to build up a bank of odd parts that may prove to be just the thing in future. Quite often 1/350 ladders make very good bridge windows in 1/700, in the absence of anything else; this was the case for *Wasp*, as can be seen in the accompanying photos.

Further details that can be added with etched brass to improve the superstructure include ladders and doors, which help to give more definition and depth; this will be particularly beneficial at the painting stage later. Other small details, such as flight-deck lights from plastic rod, help to bring a more 'cluttered' look to the area, in keeping with the subject. A number of photoetched door sets include the option to show these open; this can add a nice, busy feel to the model, showing activity taking place.

Working around the hull of *Wasp*, some areas of simplification, or incorrect interpretation of plans by the kit maker, are improved with the addition of photoetched parts. Where this is the case, the plastic is removed and the area cleaned up before adding the etched parts. It is worth taking a critical look at similar points on the kit you are building, as sometimes the interpretation of structures such as ladders, railings and other equipment may have been very simply rendered and would be much better replaced by photoetched or scratch-built parts. This is commonly the case for deck fittings such as vents, ammunition boxes, cable reels and the other varieties of clutter found on any ship.

Look closely at plans and photos to determine what that particular blob of plastic is trying to represent; getting to understand how ships work will also give you a good guess at what it is you need to replace. Ironically, it is often easier to work on a kit that has neglected to add such detail, than to work on one where it has been done poorly, since the inferior parts will have to be removed first.

Working with Photoetched Railings

Railings are best handled in sections of around 6cm: any larger and they can become difficult to manage. More importantly, when working on a resin model in particular, warm temperatures will cause the metal parts to expand slightly, often enough to cause the railing to buckle and even come free of the model.

Place the cut rail section in position on the model, and using a cocktail stick, dab a small amount of CA glue on to the model where one end of the railing is to be fixed. Position the part on to this and leave it to set: this will only take a few seconds.

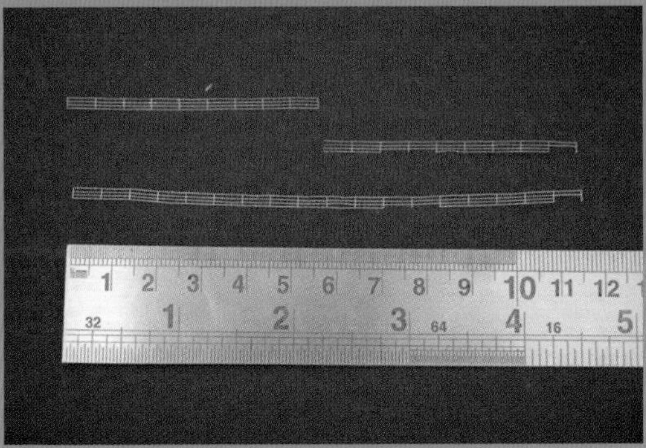

Railings cut into manageable lengths; don't worry about leaving one end without a stanchion, as this will join to the next length.

Work slowly and carefully when gluing on the railings; make sure there is no excess glue around the taped areas.

With your fingernail or whatever you find most convenient, nudge the rest of the rail into position on the deck edge. Now, brush some thinned PVA glue along the back edge of the railing and leave to dry. The PVA has enough strength to hold the railing in place, and will not leave marks along the front edge of the railing. As it retains some elasticity when set, it will allow for some expansion and contraction of the metal parts to prevent them buckling.

If necessary, work in small sections at a time, leaving the previous length to dry; this will only take a few minutes.

Adding photoetched doors, ladders, railings and other parts greatly improves on the original kit's parts.

After studying the plans, it turns out that this odd bit of 'detail' is meant to represent a hanging accommodation ladder used for boarding the ship.

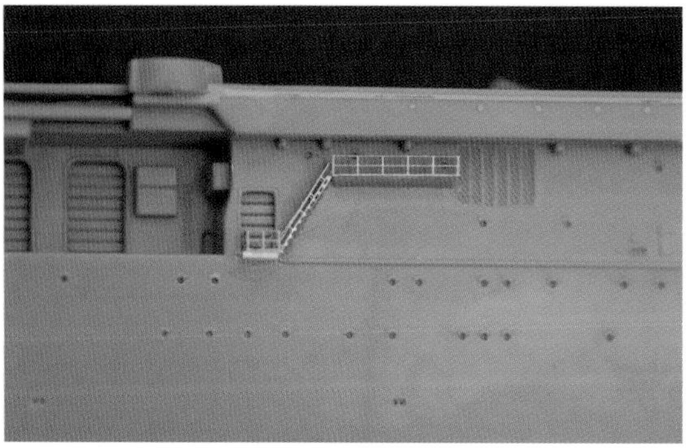

With the plastic removed, a photoetched part is put in its place, along with some small sections of railing and a plastic-card platform.

Improving Boats

Regardless of the period of the ship being modelled, somewhere there will be smaller boats used to carry crew on- and offshore, or for any number of other duties. On many kits these are neglected, but attention to detail here can greatly elevate the quality of the finished model. These can be a particular area of weakness in some plastic kits, with some rather questionably shaped pieces offered to represent on-board small boats. Thankfully with a little work these can be greatly improved, or if preferred, replaced with resin or 3D-printed versions.

Often the kit boats are quite shallow because the thwarts – the cross-pieces used to brace the sides of the boat, which also commonly serve as seats – are not sufficiently raised. This can be improved very simply using plastic strip to give more depth. Also the exact opposite can be true, and a little hollowing out of the space in between the thwarts will bring about the same result.

Some motor boats with cabins may have these represented by a solid block; however, breaking these up into separate cabins with the saw and scalpel is again a quick and easy improvement. As with splinter shields, scraping away overly thick sides is simple and effective. Photoetched oars, rudders, keels and rails can be added to increase the detail of the boats themselves, whilst etched davits can be a great improvement on kit parts.

An example of some photoetched and replacement resin parts that can be used to improve small boats and their handling equipment.

The boats on *Wasp* were not the worst, but still needed a little more detail to bring out their best. By using some etched parts, plastic strip and careful painting to add a little more depth, the boats can be much improved. Another good way to improve the appearance of boats is to use photoetched boat chocks and to remove the kit parts, which are almost always just triangular-shaped and overly thick blocks. These etched boat chocks can be tricky to use as they need to fit on the bow, stern and amidships of the boat, so getting these to fit properly and remain level can need a little adjustment. Any gaps between the boat and chock can be filled with white glue before painting.

Portholes on the motor launch are added using a black fibre-tipped pen, which is easier than trying to paint a round black point. A nice touch for completion on boats with oars is just a dab of paint where the oarlocks would be.

As the kit parts are lacking in detail, improving this can make them a focus of interest on the completed model.

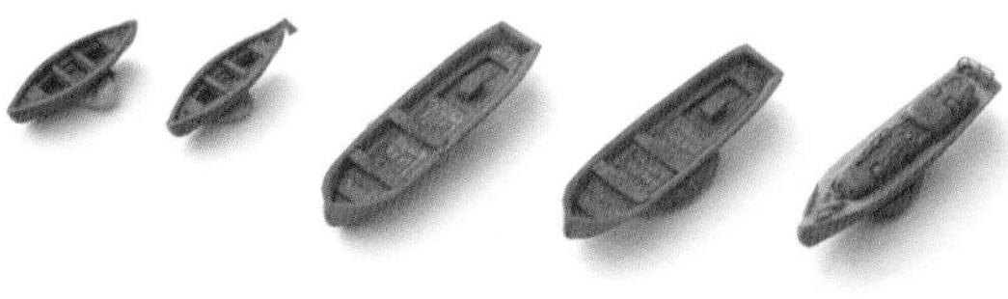

Detail painting and the addition of photoetched parts greatly improves the look of the finished boats.

Improving Aircraft

In one form or another, aircraft can be found aboard ships from the latter part of World War I up to the present day. They add interest to a model, and as a particular focus, it is worth spending a little time to improve the finished look. Once again a very wide range of photoetched parts is available in all scales, including propellers and rotors, landing gear, struts, aerials and weapons. For the determined, there are even some etched sets to reproduce canopy framing. Going a little further into 3D-printed accessories, there are some excellent weapon loads from brands such as Five Star or SSN Modellbau from Germany. Deck vehicles for aircraft carriers add a nice touch, with the range of what is available increasing all the time. Perhaps the simplest and still the most effective way to add a little finesse is to replace plastic propellers with photoetched alternatives; similarly, helicopter rotors will look much more in scale when these are used.

Most aircraft will come in the form of opaque plastic or resin, although more recent plastic kits will often include clear plastic versions, which are intended to give a better looking canopy area. In nearly all cases these will include panel lines of some sort. There is continuing debate amongst aircraft modellers as to whether these would be visible in various scales; it is safe to say that in 1/700 and 1/350 any such lines will be massively out of scale, so a better result will be achieved by filling and sanding these before progressing.

Clear plastic aircraft can first be painted with an appropriate cockpit colour, as this will show through the cockpit area on the finished model. A little Blu Tack moulded around the canopy area will help to protect it whilst the rest of the aircraft is painted. As decals will almost certainly be required, a gloss or satin paint at the painting stage can be used if available; if not, a gloss coat may be necessary.

Once the aircraft have been painted, attention turns to the canopy, and where this is not clear plastic, a decision has to be made on how best to paint it. Usually this will be a choice of black or a light blue, with the theory that the latter imitates the reflection of the sky in the glass or perspex, which would form the canopy glazing. This really is a matter of choice: both can look good when done well.

As regards painting the canopy framing, there is little more that can be done than use a fine brush,

The finished aircraft on deck; painting the canopy frame with a very fine brush needs a steady hand.

thinned paint and a steady hand. Gloss varnishing over the canopy before painting can help in removing any errors: a sharp toothpick is a good way to do this, as it will not damage the underlying paint if used gently enough. Of course the gloss will also give some reflection and help in giving the desired effect.

USING WOODEN DECKS

A relatively new addition in ship modelling is laser-cut wooden decks. These are made from thin sheets of wood, cut by laser and sometimes coloured to represent planking, so that they fit over the deck fittings and superstructures of the model. Since there will always be some degree of variation between kits of the same ship, it is important to select the right deck for the kit you have, otherwise it is quite likely that it won't fit. Most, but not all of these decks come with etched brass parts to replace the detail that has had to be removed, and are self-adhesive.

The first stage when fitting a replacement wooden deck is to remove any detail as directed by the instructions, as this will prevent it from fitting correctly. Any painting and weathering should be done to the deck before fitting, as this will be much easier than having to mask later. Quite often the colour of these wooden decks is not very accurate for the weathered teak that is commonly found on warships. This weathers to a greyish colour, whereas most decks have more of a yellow or even an orange hue.

For the USS *Wasp* model, the deck should be a reddish mahogany colour; this is produced by airbrushing thin coats of Lifecolor acrylic mahogany stain until a suitable shade results. Some light weathering in the form of thin coats of dark grey along the centre line help to create a more realistic effect. As with all ship models, the element of planning comes to the fore when deciding the best time to fit the deck. In most cases this will have to be quite early in the build or it will be impossible to fit the deck over structures already in place. Carriers allow a little more leeway in that the much simpler superstructure can be built separately and added after the deck, towards the latter stages of the build.

When the time comes to fit the deck, this has to be done with great care as any mistake in alignment means that it will have to be lifted and replaced, which of course means that the adhesive loses its strength. The result of this can be that the deck lifts at a later date and causes some unsightly bulges. A solution to this is to remove the backing layer of self-adhesive decks in stages, to score the backing sheet into sections so it can be removed more easily, then fit the deck one part at a time so that adjustments can be made as you go along.

A photo of SS Great Britain *showing the grey colour to which the deck has weathered. Ships regularly scrubbed would be less grey than this example.*

The deck now in place and weathered; the colour of US aircraft carrier decks is quite different to that found on other ships.

If there is no adhesive on the deck, a two-part epoxy would be the best solution, as this takes a few minutes to set and will form a very strong bond to the plastic. Once attached, check around the deck edges, where there may be a slight overlap that requires trimming.

PUTTING IT ALL TOGETHER

With the main hull and superstructures completed, and the small parts built and put to one side for painting, we can consider how best to proceed to complete the model. It is always best to do as much building as possible before painting, although some parts, such as railings, can be left off until painting has been completed. This is mainly to protect them from damage during the painting stage, since they can be attached using the method described previously when all painting has been completed. Later chapters will cover in detail the finishing stages of painting, weathering, making a sea base and rigging.

Painting of the model and base is done separately, although the finishing stages of the base are left until the model is mounted on it, as there are inevitably some gaps to be filled: these can be incorporated into the wake around the ship. Once the painting of the ship is completed, then this is mounted on to the baseboard using screws and

3D-printed figures give a sense of scale and movement; when placing them, consider where most activity would be.

some epoxy adhesive. The painted small parts can then be added on to the model, as there is less risk of damage to them at this stage.

To bring the model alive, a number of 3D-printed figures are added, mainly on the flight-deck, busy moving aircraft. These are quite a new addition, and are a great improvement over the photoetched ones that were previously all that was available. Care needs to be taken when removing them from the base as they are both fragile and easily lost, but once attached to some strong, double-sided tape on the wooden spill they can be airbrushed with primer, then brush painted to finish.

Once all the small details are added, the base can be finished off with the wake pattern, and final coats of paint and gloss varnish. Building the rigging is the most delicate task, and this is always left until the final stage of construction; the very last parts to be added are the radar aerials, which are easy to knock off at this point.

With all these elements complete, the model is finished and ready to take its place with the rest of the collection.

The finished model showing the camouflage scheme and weathering; the open hangar doors make a feature of the hull.

An aircraft carrier deck is a particularly busy place, so paying extra attention here adds a great deal of interest.

Chapter Five

Starting with Resin

THE DIFFERENCES IN WORKING WITH RESIN

Most modellers will be familiar with resin upgrade parts, but for ship modelling more than any other genre, full resin kits comprise a high percentage of available models. Yet there is still something of a reluctance on the part of many to move away from their tried and trusted plastic modelling techniques to learn the techniques for working with resin. Some state the higher price of resin kits as one reason for their reluctance, yet most resin kits will come with etched brass parts, and many provide turned brass or 3D-printed parts as standard. When the cost of purchasing etched brass upgrades for plastic kits is added in, there is generally very little difference in the price. Others may have tried a resin kit in the past when the hand-building of master patterns was the norm and casting techniques were not as good as now, and have been put off by the effort required to clean up parts, the poor fit, and the faults in casting.

Most modern resin kits are now designed by CAD (computer-aided design), with 3D-printed master patterns, and cast in vacuum chambers that will produce very high quality castings, generally with parts much finer than can be produced by all but the most sophisticated and expensive injection-moulding techniques. If you have some reservations about resin, learning to work in the very slightly different way that it requires will open up a huge range of subjects, and maybe make accessible that one ship model you have always wanted to build.

Resin kits are made from an entirely different material to plastic kits, the main difference being that polystyrene cements and adhesives will not work. These rely on melting the plastic to join the parts, so will not be effective on resins, which need another type of adhesive that relies on forming a bond between the two parts. In most cases this means using cyanoacrylate (CA) adhesive, or 'superglue'. For small parts PVA glue can be used, but mainly we will be working with CA adhesive on resin, so this can be taken as the default adhesive.

The resins used for casting models are not all the same; they vary from some that are quite brittle and even crumbly, to those with a softer, soapier texture. As with most things in life, neither extreme is particularly good, and quality resin casts will fall midway in between, neither too hard to work nor too soft to distort easily. However, the nature of the material means that it will always be more brittle than plastic and more prone to damage, both during construction and as the kit is received. Because of this, some small repair work on parts is to be expected, as are loose parts, given the usual fineness of attachment points.

Really then, there is not a lot of difference between plastic and resin kits, except that a little more work will sometimes be required to clean up parts, the adhesives used are different, and there are some considerations of health and safety that differ from working with plastic.

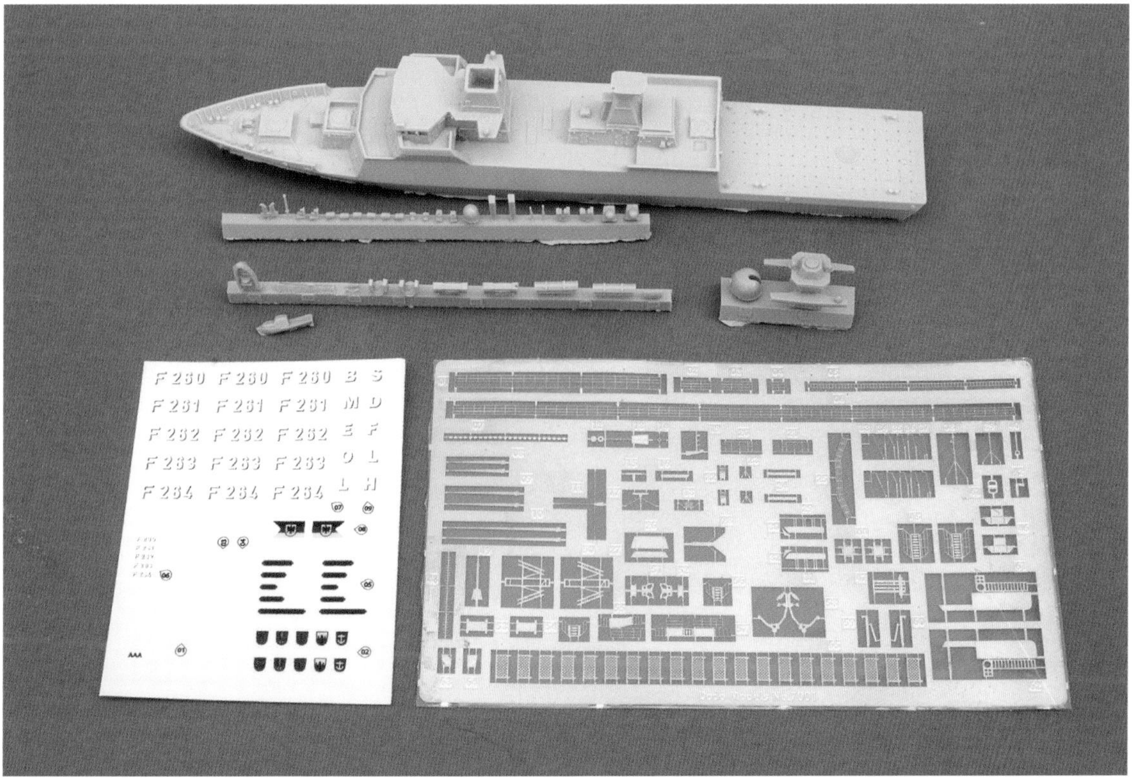

This kit of a Braunschweig-class corvette from Dodo Models is typical of modern resin kits, designed by computer and finely cast from a 3D-printed prototype.

HEALTH AND SAFETY WHEN WORKING WITH RESIN

The type of resin used for model kits is polyurethane: the downside of polyurethane is that it contains isocyanates, which are toxic, and in the form of dust that can be inhaled. Exposure to resin dust can cause severe respiratory illnesses and is therefore to be avoided. Where possible avoid sanding resin parts; instead, proceed by cutting, paring and scraping them with a scalpel as this will produce large fragments that do not risk being easily inhaled.

It should be noted that exposure to any dust, including that from polystyrene kits, carries an element of risk; therefore when sanding any parts it is best to do so in a well-ventilated room using an extraction system if you have one. If not, then spraying the parts with water will help to keep down any dust, and a face mask or, if a lot of sanding is required, a respirator is strongly recommended. Pay attention to the modelling area when cleaning up, and use a damp kitchen towel to remove any dust from the working area.

Since CA adhesives will be used for much of the time whilst working with resin, a mention must be made of the health and safety issues of these. The risk of this product bonding to skin is well known: this is because it will set when in contact with moisture, and if this happens, hot soap and water will be needed to remove it. If working closely there is a danger of it splashing into the eye, which is a much more serious problem requiring hospital treatment – some eye protection is certainly helpful if this should be the case, though fortunately many of us wear spectacles, which are adequate for this purpose. A spillage of a large amount of CA adhesive will give off strong fumes, so again, working in a well-ventilated area is to be recommended.

One little known fact is that CA adhesive can react with some natural fibres, paper or similar organic-based materials, and produce an exothermic reaction that can generate enough heat to cause a very nasty burn – in extreme cases it can cause combustion of the material.

There are more issues to consider when working with resin, but, as with any potentially harmful practice, the only adjustment that is needed is to take the necessary precautions and slightly alter working methods to take account of the hazards.

REMOVING AND CLEANING UP PARTS

The process of resin casting involves various methods of getting liquid resin into a mould, which is then left to harden. This requires somewhere for the resin to be introduced, and in order to prevent air pockets, somewhere for air to escape. In both cases there will be a plug of resin in the part that needs to be cleaned off. There may be some roughness around the bottom of larger parts, and casting seams also often require work – again, this is normal and just related to the process of resin casting. Occasionally a part that should have a flat bottom will have become concave due to the resin shrinking as it cools; this can be filled with Milliput or similar before sanding flat.

With more modern resin kits, removal of any casting stubs is the same as for removing parts from an injection-moulded sprue: trim as closely as possible with the scalpel, and finish off with a few swipes of the sanding stick. Some parts may be attached to a block, which can be removed with a razor saw, then cleaned up as previously. Should there be any gaps to fill, the same fillers as for plastic kits can largely be used, apart from liquid plastic fillers, which will not adhere to the surface well. Milliput, gap-filling CA adhesive and the Mr Surfacer brand of liquid fillers are some of the fillers appropriate for using on resin.

Resin is formed by the mixing of two parts, which then react to form a solid compound; during this mixing air bubbles are usually formed, and if not removed by placing in a vacuum chamber, may still be present when the resin solidifies. Similarly,

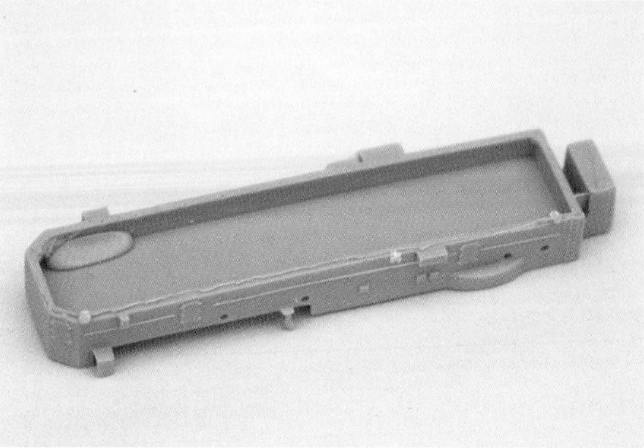

As with injection plastic kits, resin parts will have some casting plugs that need to be removed, and the part must be generally tidied up before use.

This 1/700 kit of the submarine USS Nautilus *by OKB Grigorov has a casting block that can be removed with a razor saw, or scored through with a scalpel or scriber.*

Removing Resin Parts from the Casting Wafer

Older-style resin kits often featured parts cast on to a wafer or block; this is less frequent with more recent kits, but is still sometimes found. This needs to be removed cleanly so that the parts are even and not sanded more on one side than another, which will, of course, affect the fit and look of the model. The best way to do this so as to avoid damage to the part is to sand it away, of course taking care to reduce the amount of dust produced. Wet-and-dry or silicon carbide paper is used for this; progressively finer grades can be employed, depending on the thickness of the wafer and how much sanding needs to be done. With very thin wafers, such as those found on Combrig kits, very little work is needed so a fine grade can be used from the start.

The technique is similar to that used for vacform models: using a fine felt-tip or similar pen, draw around the part as closely as possible to it. Trim away the excess around the part to leave a couple of millimetres of the wafer.

Using a little water on the paper, sand down the part in a circular motion; keep this even so as to prevent too much wear on one side or another. Alternating three clockwise with three anti-clockwise movements should keep progress even and steady. Check the part after each of these passes; when the marked line is visible through the resin, switch to a finer grade and complete the removal of the wafer. You should now have a flat and even part ready to be used.

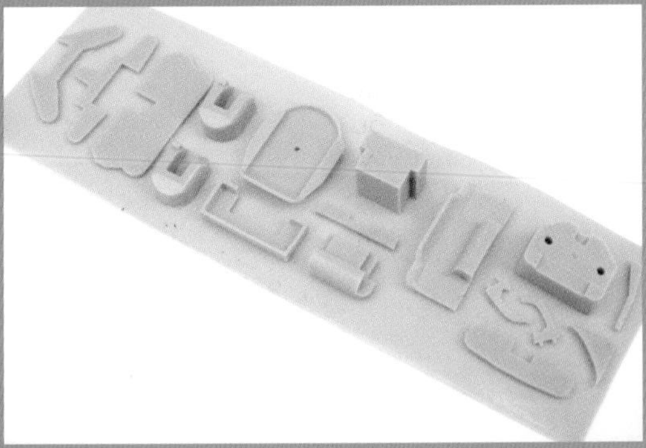

Parts that come on a very thin casting wafer can be removed easily with a little sanding on fine-grade wet-and-dry paper taped to the cutting mat.

Marking out around the edge of the part will help to show how close it is to being removed.

Work carefully and do not put more pressure on one side of the part than the other; the black line should then appear evenly around the edge of the wafer.

if a vacuum chamber is not used when the resin is poured into the mould, bubbles will be left behind, often in the corner angles. This can be a time-consuming problem to resolve, especially in corners, as a hard filler is needed to keep the corners looking neat. Thick CA adhesive can be used here, as this can be trimmed and sanded to shape and will be hard enough to retain a sharp angle.

One good way to make a filler is to mix CA adhesive with a talcum or baking powder, as this forms a very strong filler that can be sanded to a fine finish. For a larger repair, some Milliput first fixed into place with a dab of CA adhesive is a good starting point, but there should be few occasions when such heavy-duty repair is necessary.

Most modern resin kits will come with parts on a sprue or on a wafer, although there are still some that can have thick casting blocks attached to the hull; these can be difficult to remove without damaging the part. The best method is to use a vice, placing the top of the casting block level with the top edges of the vice so it can act as a guide. Using a fine-toothed saw, the block can be cut away to release the part, taking care as usual over dust, as this can produce quite a large amount.

WORKING WITH RESIN

Building a resin kit is really little different from an injection plastic one, and it is surprising that so many people seem reluctant to work with it, considering the great number of potential subjects the medium offers. The only real difference is that parts may require a little more cleaning, and different adhesives must be used, which requires a small alteration to working practices.

CA adhesives will generally be used, and because for most types setting time is a matter of a few seconds, test fitting to get the correct placement of parts is essential, as it will be difficult to alter their position or remove them once the adhesive has set. Clearly for parts such as superstructures that require precise alignment this is not very satisfactory. In this case moving to a two-part epoxy adhesive is a good choice, as setting time is in the order of a few minutes and the bond is just as strong. Slow-setting CA is also available and can be used in a similar fashion.

When working with CA in general, use a non-porous surface to dab on a small amount of adhesive, then with a cocktail stick place a small drop on the desired location on the model. This is preferable to adding adhesive to the part, as it is easy to add too much and cause it to overflow; also it will allow for the part to be positioned more accurately. An overspill from the use of CA can sometimes be cleaned off with a cotton bud soaked in some nail-varnish remover, or any acetone-based fluid. Failing that, scraping with the scalpel blade and a little tidy up with the sanding stick is generally enough.

Thin resin parts such as gun barrels, davits and masts are prone to distortion as a result of cooling after being released from the mould; they are also more brittle than plastic and more easily damaged. For that reason these may need to be replaced with etched or turned brass parts; many kits do in any case now include these as standard. Many resin kits do not include masts for this reason, and these have to be constructed from brass rod or aftermarket turned brass. We will take a look at how these can be used in the next chapter, following the build of a resin ship kit.

Chapter Six

Building a Resin Model Kit

THE STARLING MODELS KIT OF HMS *NADDER*

For our resin kit build the subject will be the 1/350 model of the River class frigate HMS *Nadder* produced by Starling Models. The River class frigates were built in large numbers for convoy escort and were operated mainly by the Royal Navy, the Royal Canadian Navy and the Royal Australian Navy in World War II. This was a successful design that formed the basis for the later Loch class anti-submarine and Bay class anti-aircraft frigates.

The kit is fairly typical of the newer generation of resin kits that have been designed using computer-modelling software to produce a 3D-printed pattern, which is then used for resin casting. Included in the kit are resin parts, a brass photoetched fret, turned brass barrels and mast, and a decal sheet. The parts are free of casting blocks, and the smaller parts are attached to a sprue, although a number of these are loose in the bag where the fine attachment points have broken. Along with the high quality instruction sheet, the completeness of the kit is becoming commonplace for resin kits.

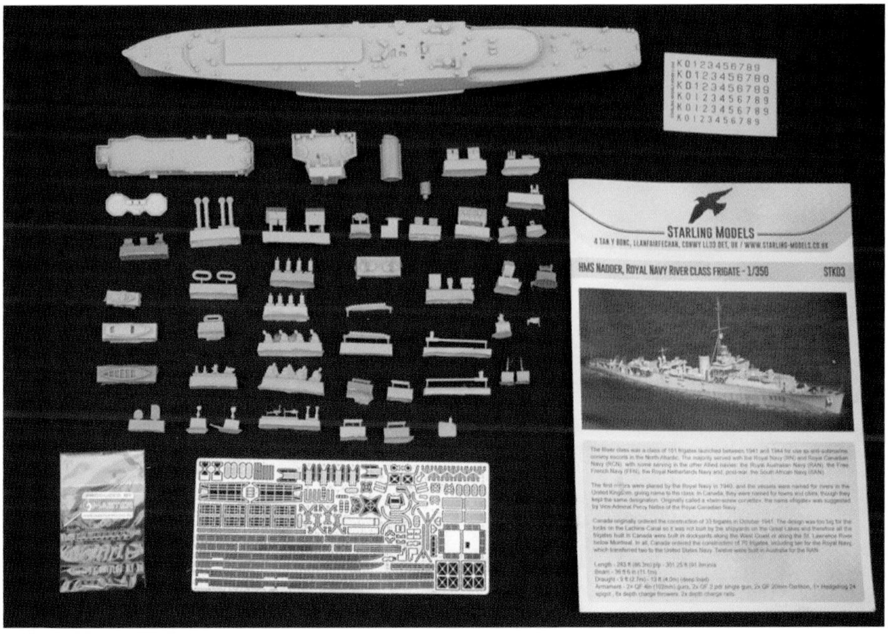

The Starling Models kit of HMS Nadder *includes most of what is required to complete the model, as is often the case with modern resin kits.*

PREPARATION

Some resin kits come with a greasy mould release on the surface: this needs to be cleaned off by soaking in warm water with a little detergent. Areas around the hull sides can be cleaned with an old toothbrush, but take great care in any area where detail can be damaged. As with plastic kits, in many cases this step is not necessary unless the mould release is heavy and likely to cause problems at the painting stage later: if it is not, it may be best not to bother.

Resin does have a tendency to bend, either as a result of being removed from the mould a little too quickly, or where parts are long and thin; unfortunately this can particularly be the case for waterline hulls. Older kits that have been stored for some time, especially in warm temperatures, may start to bend so there is a bow in the middle. Do not attempt to straighten this without first warming up the resin to make it more pliable, as it will crack. To warm it, boil some water and let it cool for a few minutes, then pour this into a flat dish or tray large enough to hold the length of the hull. Place the model into this for a minute or two and the resin will soften slightly. Carefully push the model down on to a flat surface, and it will quickly cool and retain the corrected shape.

Sometimes a resin part may be bent and will need some attention; do not try to force the part into place before warming it, as it will probably break.

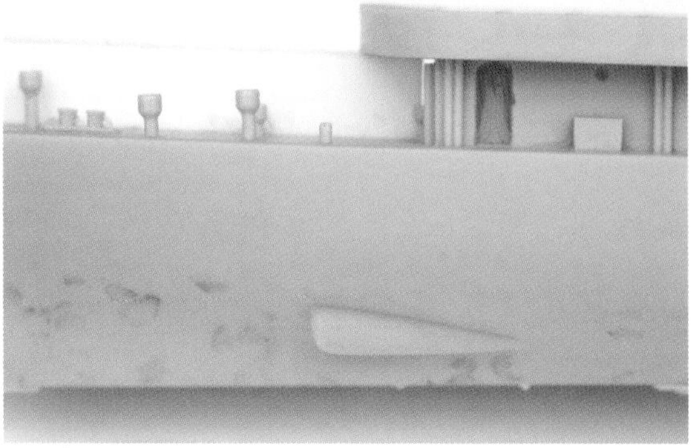

With the part warmed and gently pushed back into place, it is a good idea to ensure it stays that way by using a temporary support.

It may be necessary to repeat this a few times, especially when the hull is deep. In all cases it is best to be on the safe side and to make sure that any hull that has to be treated in this way is firmly attached to a solid base once completed to prevent it reverting to its previous state. In fact this is one reason for making full-hull resin models, in that the likelihood of the part bending over time is almost eliminated due to the much more solid block of resin.

Sometimes parts other than the hull may have distorted slightly – one small area on the *Nadder* kit needed this attention. The gun-deck platform astern that extends over the quarterdeck was bent slightly downwards, and this can happen with fine resin casting. Using the hot water trick, the platform was pushed slightly upwards and a piece of thick plastic card cut to size inserted underneath to ensure the desired angle was achieved; it was then left to cool.

CLEANING UP PARTS

Due to the casting process, flash may be found around some parts, but this is generally very fine and can easily be trimmed away with the scalpel. Working slowly around the model, any flash is removed with a fresh scalpel blade, and any other larger parts similarly treated. The parts of a resin kit tend to come in three ways: on a casting wafer, as we saw in the last chapter, on a sprue very similar to a plastic kit, or sometimes already separated in a bag. In the last two cases it is simply a matter of cleaning off the resin from the attachment point, similar to cleaning the sprue attachment from a plastic kit.

Where small parts on plastic kits require replacement this generally comes in the form of resin aftermarket items, often made available separately from an original kit. Checking over the parts for the HMS *Nadder* kit, there is nothing in the way of aftermarket replacements required; all that will be added are some crew figures to bring some life to the completed model.

The hull is typical of resin kits in that a lot of small detail is already in place; this reduces the number of small parts that have to be assembled, and makes building time much quicker. Having detail such as the small vents cast on to the hull is one of the advantages of a resin kit; in plastic this would be difficult to replicate and the parts would either have to be separate, or much simplified and therefore incorrect. This does mean, however, that some of these parts may be broken off at some point; usually they will be somewhere in the kit bag or box and can be reattached.

ASSEMBLY

Planning construction of the model can now begin; as ever the ease of painting is the determining factor. The River class frigates, in common with many small warships of the period, had bridge wings overhanging part of the deck and supported with lattice work. Clearly this will be the most difficult part of the painting process, and construction needs to work around that problem. Painting everything first and then attaching the parts is not ideal, since any mistake in placing the part will damage the paintwork. This is especially the case for resin kits, since most of the time CA adhesive will be used and this will tear off the underlying paint if it needs to be removed.

The answer is to proceed with the build until the point where adding any more to the main hull will make painting too difficult. In the case of HMS *Nadder*, this means adding the main forward superstructure, lattice supports, funnel, and any other details that would be tricky to fit at a later date, such as the float racks located on the sides of the forward and aft superstructures. Railings have also been added at this stage since they would be tricky to position around the lattice supports and boat stowage.

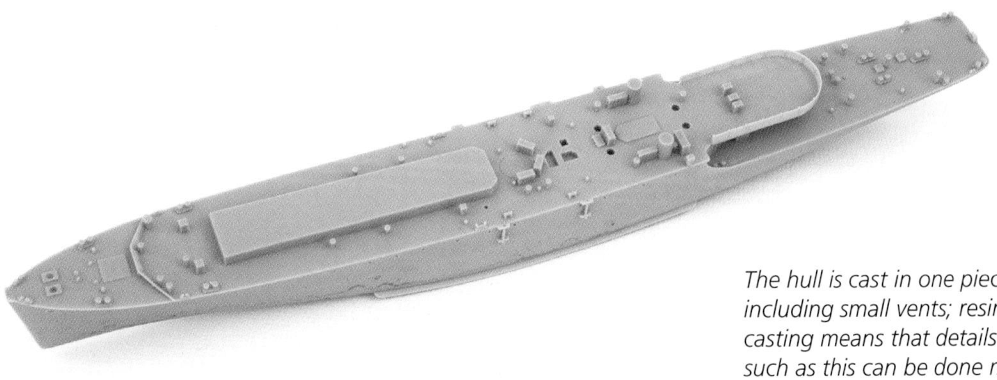

The hull is cast in one piece, including small vents; resin casting means that details such as this can be done more accurately than in plastic.

The bridge can now be built as a sub-assembly, and the remainder of the parts completed as required and attached to wooden craft sticks ready for painting. Some of these can be left on the sprue, especially parts such as the depth-charge launchers and reloads, since the attachment point to the sprue is where the part will need to be glued. The same applies to the boats, although care needs to be taken when painting these to ensure that the lower hulls are properly painted as well.

PAINTING THE CAMOUFLAGE

Now that most of the parts are assembled, painting can commence with a primer coat. (We will cover the actual techniques of painting and weathering in much greater detail in the next chapter.) Priming is especially important on resin kits, as any residue of mould release will mean that paint will not adhere well. At this stage priming also gives the opportunity to pick up on any small errors or marks. It is particularly helpful to tidy up any mistakes with

Small parts and railings have been added to the hull, though masts have been left off at this stage as they would be easily damaged.

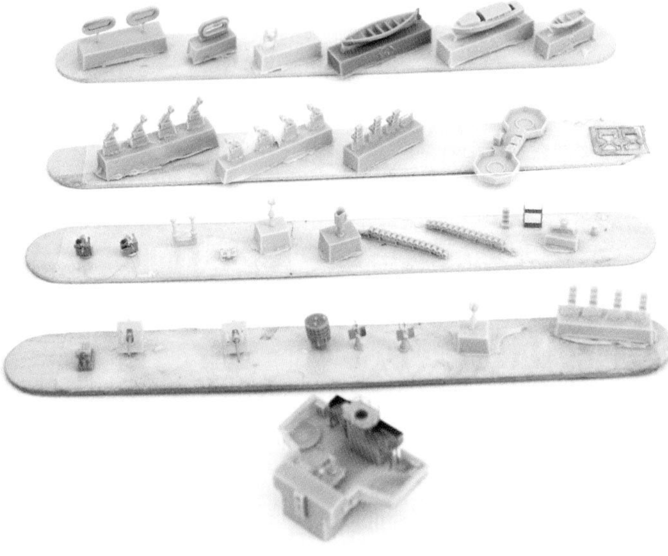

Set all your small parts to one side, and ideally in a closed box to prevent loss or damage; painting is much easier when they are attached to a base.

Working with Railings

Some kits, such as the Starling Models kit of HMS *Nadder*, have notches on the railings where they are to be folded, which makes placement much easier; when using generic railing sets a little more work is required to ensure the railing lengths needed are the correct size. A very useful tool for this is a digital calliper: first, measure the distance of railing required on the model, then transfer this to the section of railing to be cut. Cutting the railing at a stanchion will probably mean – unless you are lucky – that one end of the part will be open, and this will need to be carefully glued on to the next railing section to close the gap. White glue is again good for this as it will fill the gap and shrink once dried.

To avoid errors and wasting etched parts, a calliper can be used to give the exact length needed. The measurement is not important as long as the correct distance is held.

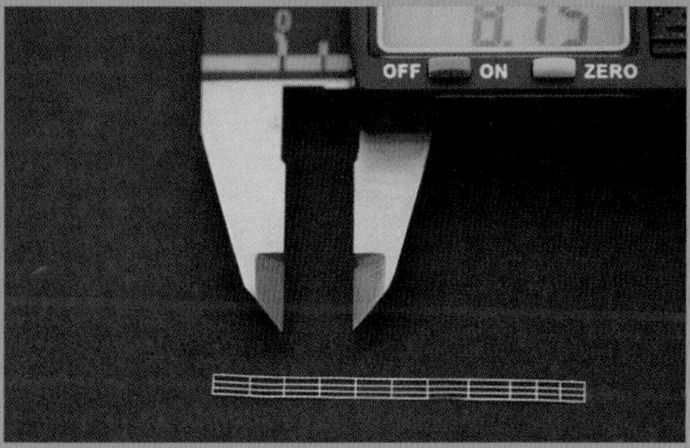

Transfer the measurement to the part and cut off the required length; small curved nail scissors are very useful for cutting off any tags from the railing.

At times complex shapes of railing will be required, and it is tempting to try to fold a section of rail to fit all in one piece. This is not often a success, as making more than a couple of bends is almost certain to lead to error, which will only be increased the more bends that are made. A better approach is to make at most two bends in a section and then attach this to the model before going on to the next. Similarly, curved sections can be very tricky to get right; rolling a round rod of an appropriate size will give an even curve.

The complicated railing sections around the bow of this Russian gunboat have been made with several small lengths; work is still in progress on this model.

Most ships will have two different types of railing: those along the hull edge are usually stanchions with chain, while on earlier ships, ropes form the actual barrier. Along the edge of superstructures these would more usually be solid, more along the lines of a metal fence. This does make a difference when deciding how these should ideally be modelled: whilst it is common to find upper railings without stanchions at corners, as these are basically metal tubing and do not require support, it would not be realistic to show railings in this way along the hull side. Some careful cutting and fitting may be required at times to achieve a sharp and accurate look to complicated sections of railing, so that each corner is marked with a stanchion. Using railings with closer stanchion spacing is a great help when it comes to making such intricate details.

railing: these can be filled with a little Mr Surfacer, then carefully cleaned up with a cotton bud and a little thinner to give a nice clean join.

Once the primer is dry and any errors corrected and tidied up, the base camouflage colour is painted; this is an off-white, as part of the Western Approaches scheme the ship wore. Once masked off, the second colour, a pale blue called B55, is airbrushed on. Both colours are Lifecolor acrylics; the white is used only sparingly under the overhangs to give a little shade in these areas and prevent the colour looking too monotone. Although the model will be put on a sea base, the plan is for this to be showing rough waves, so some of the lower hull will be visible. This is similarly masked off and painted; the boot topping (the line marking the waterline on the hull) will be added later using black decal strip. Some details can be picked out at this stage, such as the black of the funnel cap, since airbrush painting is now complete.

The separate smaller parts and sub-assemblies are painted at the same time, and any small details requiring a different colour are picked out to help break up the overall look of the model. Paying attention to small details at this stage can greatly increase the visual interest, especially if the colour scheme is a one-colour grey. This would be even more important should the model require the overall dark blue schemes of some USN ships in the later stages of World War II, as decks were also painted dark blue. The different colours of the boats, carley floats (life rafts), depth charges and other smaller details add contrast to the light camouflage scheme and greatly improve the realism of the finished model.

In the larger scales, paying a little attention to the ship's boats is a good way to add some variation, since they would often have areas of unpainted but varnished wood. The open boats are painted in a variety of wood shades from the very useful Lifecolor Weathered Wood set, with some oars added to the whaler from plastic rod. Using small-diameter rounded rod for oars gives a better impression than flat etched parts, and the ends can be flattened with pliers to create the blade. For the motorboat, the small side windows are inked in using a 0.5mm-tip marker pen; this is much easier than trying to use a paintbrush, and gives a much sharper edge.

The task of painting the main colours is complete, and larger parts previously set aside are now added to build up the structure of the ship.

A fine, fibre-tipped black pen is easier to control than a brush when painting windows; the same can be used for portholes.

A LITTLE EXTRA DETAIL

Etched parts do add a great deal of detail, but sometimes these can be better represented by replacing them with something more three-dimensional. Typical examples are davits, which often come as etch, but in larger scales these look too flat on the completed model. Replacement boat davits for *Nadder* are made from brass rod bent round a paintbrush handle, with the shape matched to the etched part.

A nice detail is to add some 'glass' to the searchlights. This is a quite simple and effective procedure: drill out the centre of the part – the tip of the drill will give a concave hole, which is then filled with a small blob of white glue. Leave this to dry, and repeat a few times until a dome builds up, creating the impression of the glass lens of the searchlight.

The deck can now be painted, and this is hand brushed; Royal Navy ships of the period often had a variety of deck coverings to prevent the crew slipping. At first this was a linoleum covering called corticene, which was a reddish-brown colour. Later this was changed to the harder-wearing semtex, a compound that was poured on to the deck, which was initially a pale brown colour but later green. The early semtex varied in colour and of course would change during use from the effects of the sun, salt and dirt from the activities of the crew. In this case Lifecolor acrylics were again used, this time Italian Sand, which is a good representation of the semtex colour – there is no accurate match in the range. This is thinned a little with their own brand of thinner to prevent streaking; a small amount of Winsor and Newton acrylic retarder also helps to prevent it drying too quickly and forming ridges.

Brass rod is often a better material for parts such as boat davits, as these can appear flat and two-dimensional; in this case 0.4mm rod is used.

Searchlights and any other part requiring a glass effect can be effectively replicated by gradually building up layers of white glue, with a little gloss varnish to finish if required.

The build progresses with alternate stages of painting and the addition of small parts, leaving those most fragile to the last.

As ever with brush painting, several thin coats are needed, as rushing this stage can produce a poor finish and detract from the final model. Once dry, a little weathering can be added around the most heavily used areas such as the weapons and bridge; a little dry pigment is ideal for this.

FINAL STAGES TO FINISH

With the main painting complete, the sub-assembly and small parts can gradually be added; the most fragile and easily damaged should be left until the end stages of completion, as long as they are straightforward enough in terms of placement, such as the light AA weapons. As with many resin kits, the bridge location is marked out on the deck but does not include any location pins. Using CA adhesive in this situation is less than ideal since the bridge needs to be aligned correctly with the lattice supports already in place. Although slow-setting CA is available, a two-part epoxy adhesive is preferable since it will set in around five minutes, which gives plenty of time to make any adjustments to the positioning.

The last stage of construction should always be the masts, as these are most likely to be damaged as work progresses around the model. *Nadder* has a simple tripod-type mast, and this is made of brass rod. Since there is not much rigging the rod can be glued using CA adhesive or epoxy, as this will give a sufficiently strong bond to hold under the tension applied by the rigging material. Epoxy is again a better choice since the mast needs to be positioned accurately: at 90 degrees amidships but at a slight angle towards the stern. Incorrectly placed masts are a common mistake in otherwise quality ship

Construction is almost complete; masts are added towards the end of the building phase. The model still looks very clean, but that won't last for long.

models, so it is very much worth taking time with this part of the model.

Final touches to the model before putting it on to the base include the addition of anchor chains: these can be bought in several sizes, determined by the number of links per centimetre. The smallest of these is sixteen links per centimetre, which is suitable for larger 1/700 models, while ten links per centimetre is suitable for 1/350. These will come in either raw brass or copper colour, or

If you are willing to go the extra mile for your model, items such as 3D-printed stud anchor chain raise the level of detail.

The completed model shows how the weathering is enough to give the impression of a hard-working ship, but it is not overdone, which would be unrealistic.

Showing the model in a rough sea state adds an element of drama, giving it movement and life.

otherwise already blackened; both need painting with an airbrush, or to be given a little weathering to tone them down. Once in place they look very effective, and much better than an etched alternative.

Recently arrived in the ever-expanding range of 3D-printed products are chains with the correct stud – this is a bar that goes across the middle of the chain to prevent it becoming tangled. This type of chain is used on all ships. For model use it is manufactured by YXModel from China and does require painting before use. Once in place the result is exceptionally good, and is an example of how 3D printing can produce items previously impossible to replicate with traditional injection and casting techniques.

The model is now rigged to finish construction, and ready to be married with the sea base; these last steps will be covered in detail in later chapters.

IN CONCLUSION

Building a resin kit is a little different to a plastic one, but while there are some elements that are slightly more difficult, there are others that are much easier. With a little care and attention given to the risk of resin dust and the need for different adhesives, resin kits really do not greatly differ from injection plastic kits. Certainly in the case of modern resin kits, more and finer detail is cast on to the parts so the need for the work of removing and improving weak areas is often much less. Perhaps the perceived greater cost means that modellers are less willing to risk the occasional failures that we all have. With so much choice on the market, there is the chance to try your hand at an inexpensive kit to get some experience before progressing to the more complex multimedia kits.

Chapter Seven

Painting and Weathering

There cannot be any doubt that the modern-day modeller has at his or her disposal a greater variety of choice than ever before. It seems that every aircraft or armoured vehicle that has ever existed has a kit available in some form or other, and manufacturers have now got to the point of even producing kits of subjects that never got further than some rough ideas on a drawing board. If the exact variation the modeller wants to produce isn't available, no doubt there will be an aftermarket conversion set to be cut and pasted on to a donor kit. Because of this there is usually no need to do more than assemble a variety of parts, so much of the emphasis has moved away from construction to painting and finishing. The far wider number of ships that remain without a kit of any sort means that in our particular area of the hobby world, this does not always ring quite so true, but generally the principle still applies.

The result of this is that there are more products available than ever before for painting and weathering, and this can become a rather bewildering choice. There is also the risk when mixing and matching products that they may not be compatible and may react with each other, causing damage to the paint job.

Ship models are by their nature complex, with many small parts that are at risk of being damaged during the painting process, and plenty of nooks and crannies that are difficult to reach. Decks are almost always a different colour to the hull and superstructure, so there are potentially a lot of areas in which mistakes can be made. Working in smaller scales a paint smudge that would go unnoticed on a tank or aircraft model becomes a glaring error. For these reasons most, although not all, ship modellers will resort to using an airbrush so as to produce a smooth and consistent finish, to cover small and intricate parts satisfactorily, and so they can reach parts of the model that would be tricky using a traditional paintbrush. Painting the model by hand brush can be done, of course, but it requires a great deal of skill and refined technique to do this to a high standard.

Once the basics of using an airbrush have been acquired, it is an easier method to produce a high quality finish more quickly. Airbrushing techniques for models are in fact a subject that requires a book on its own to cover, an excellent one being *Airbrushing Scale Model Aircraft* by Robin Carpenter (2018, The Crowood Press Ltd), with many of the techniques included being equally applicable to other genres of modelling. Some basic principles that have been learned the hard way are nevertheless worth covering here.

AIRBRUSH EQUIPMENT

At the simplest level, to start airbrushing two things are needed: an airbrush and a source of air. Beyond this things get a little more complicated, as there is, of course, a lot of choice and it is important to avoid the pitfalls and not buy a piece of equipment unsuited to the task.

Airbrushes

Airbrushes broadly fall into one of two types: single or double action. Single-action airbrushes have a trigger that controls the flow of air, and an adjustable screw at the back end that controls the flow of paint. They are simpler, cheaper and easy to use, but offer less control than a double-action airbrush. Given that most of the use for an airbrush in ship modelling is to give a smooth and consistent coverage of paint, this type is fine for the job we need it to do.

Double-action airbrushes have a trigger that moves up and down and backwards and forwards: the down pressure controls the amount of air, pulling backwards controls the amount of paint. Again, these usually have a screw at the rear to control the maximum volume of paint. These are more difficult to use but allow more control, which is important when painting very fine details.

Either type of airbrush can be used and will produce excellent results, though if the budget stretches to the more expensive double-action type, this is the best option. The other main consideration is the size of the needle, as this will dictate the amount of paint that can be put through the airbrush. An ideal size for the sort of work we will need it for is a 0.3mm needle, which gives good coverage for painting the hull and other large areas, but also allows fine lines should they be needed. Smaller than this and it becomes a slow process to spray a large area, while bigger than 0.3mm means that fine control is more difficult. Most airbrush specialists will have a chart showing which model is best suited to the needs of the modeller, given that airbrushes are now commonly used in such diverse fields as cosmetics and cake decoration – so with reference to this kind of information mistakes can be avoided.

As with most things, though, it is a matter of personal preference, and the best way to decide on the model that will suit you is first to do a little research as to which airbrush will suit your particular needs, then try to visit a model show where you can try out the different brands. There is no real comparison to trying out an airbrush in person: how it feels in the hand, and how comfortable and easy it is to use, will really make the decision for you regarding the one to buy.

Air Supply

The next decision is the choice of air supply; at its most basic this can be from an aerosol can, but these are not ideal as the air from them is not consistent – they are wasteful, and in the long run more expensive than a compressor. Once again be careful here that you buy something suitable for the task: two essential requirements for a compressor for model painting are pressure control and a moisture trap. Most airbrush work will be carried out in the 15–25psi range, so the compressor needs to be able to deliver this with the option to increase or decrease the pressure.

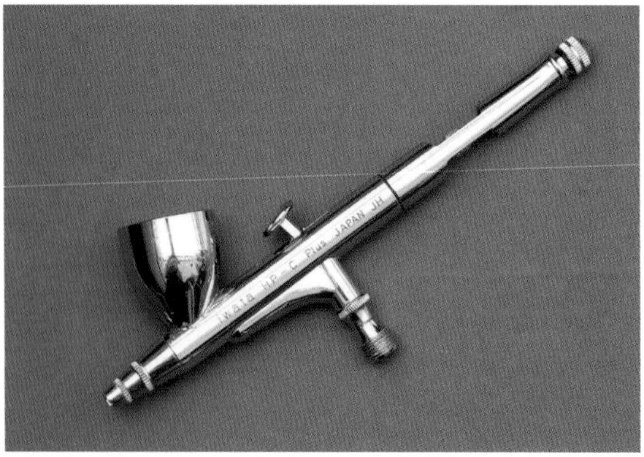

The Iwata HP-C is a typical double-action airbrush: it is reliable, easy to clean and maintain, and is available at a reasonable price.

A basic air compressor, and a more expensive model from Iwata. The basic model is fine for the job but can be noisy, and will need to be left to cool down during a long painting session.

A moisture trap will stop water getting into the air supply and then into the airbrush: if this happens it will result in splattering or drops of water on the paint job, which will leave spots when they dry.

At the budget end, a perfectly serviceable compressor can be found to do the job; as the price increases, the more sophisticated models tend to be quieter, smoother running and easier to work with.

CHOICE OF PAINT TYPE

There is a bewildering array of paint brands available to the modeller, but these break down broadly into three types: enamel, acrylic and lacquer, and all have their advantages and disadvantages. Our need is for a paint that can be used equally well for both airbrush and hand painting. The reason for this, and more so than for other styles of modelling, is that most ships require a combination of airbrushing and hand painting – the close spacing and intricacy of the various decks and superstructures means that mistakes are inevitable. Some touching up towards the end of painting will always be required, which means hand brushing. Airbrushing is the preferred method for the majority of painting tasks, so a paint that will both hand brush and airbrush well is the best choice.

Enamel

Enamel is the 'traditional' model paint, oil-based and thinned with white spirit or similar, and cleaned with the same. These paints have the advantage of being relatively similar in that they will all work well with thinners such as white spirit, although a little experimentation will be needed to find the best results. Where possible use the thinners produced by the brand, as this is the most reliable route, although it may prove a little more expensive.

As an oil-based product, enamels, once thoroughly dried, produce a tough finish that adheres well to primer, as it bonds with any underlying layers. This means they are good for painting complex camouflage schemes where a lot of masking is required, since there is less risk of the paint lifting once the masking tape is removed. Enamels do need to be stored properly with the lids cleaned off to prevent any air getting in, which will harden the paint. It has to be said that wastage of enamel paint is generally much higher than for acrylics, which tend to be easier to store.

Although in general the range of available colours specifically for naval models is more limited than for acrylics, Sovereign Hobbies produce a range of enamel paint that is specifically and accurately made for this purpose. Their Colourcoats range includes a great number of paints backed by thorough research, and these are highly recommended. A number of convenient packs for specific periods or even ships are available from them; their Graf Spee set is used in this book.

The main issues against the use of enamels are longer drying times, smell and – Colourcoats apart – a reduced range of brands and colours. Enamels really need at least twenty-four hours to dry properly before recoating, or ideally longer before masking, which can greatly

The Colourcoats enamel set for Graf Spee *includes seven 14ml tins; this is a very convenient way to build a correct colour set for the model.*

slow down progress on the model. Thinners and cleaners for oil-based paints are all strong smelling, especially when working in a confined space. The same precautions should be used in this case as when producing resin dust – indeed, for any painting with an airbrush it is advisable to use some form of paint booth, mask and, if the budget will run to it, a fume extraction system.

Acrylics

Acrylics have become the more popular choice for the modeller in recent years. Although slightly more difficult to use than enamels in some ways, there is a much wider choice available in terms of both brands and available colours. The term 'acrylic' is used for a wide variety of paint types; some of these can be thinned with water, others, such as Tamiya, are not water based and water cannot be used as a thinner. As with enamels, most brands will have their own thinners available, and until you get used to the characteristics of the individual brand, the safest route is to use those.

In general acrylic paints are fast drying and odourless, and many can be used equally well through an airbrush or when painting by hand. However, they are not as durable as enamels, different brands cannot usually be mixed, cleaning can sometimes be a little more difficult, and their faster drying time means that the airbrush needle clogs more quickly and will need to be cleaned regularly during painting. Cleaning is simply achieved by removing the paint nozzle and carefully wiping the needle tip with a cotton bud dampened with an appropriate thinner. Acrylic paints are not as durable as enamels and can be easily damaged by rubbing or scratching; therefore if acrylics have been used, greater care is needed when working around the model.

Our need to have a paint that can be hand brushed and airbrushed means that brands such as Tamiya, which cannot be hand brushed, are much more difficult to use, although some modellers do manage perfectly well with them. There are fewer colours and sets made specifically for ship modelling; of these Lifecolor make some very useful and colourful box sets for British, German, US, Japanese and Italian ships. This is an excellent brand of paint that covers well and can be used with an airbrush or hand brushes with equal success. Similar boxed sets are available from AK Interactive and Vallejo.

Acrylic paint sets from Lifecolor; these useful sets boxed by subject area contain 22ml bottles, and their own brand thinner and cleaner both make the painting job simpler.

Lacquer

Lacquer paint is becoming more popular; initially the use of these was confined to metallic finishes, but more typical colours are now available. The difference between enamel, acrylic and lacquer lies in the solvent used to carry the paint pigments; metallic lacquers are cellulose based, while colour lacquers tend to use a less aggressive solvent. Because of this they don't smell as strongly, but the difficulty of hand brushing and the limited range of colours largely discounts them for our purposes.

PAINT COLOUR ACCURACY AND THE SCALE EFFECT

Much is made of the accuracy of paint colours for modelling, but is this in fact an issue? Of course when painting it is important to have the correct shade and hue of the original colour, but other factors come into play when considering accuracy. Modellers refer to something called the scale effect, which basically means that viewing a 1/700 model from 1 foot away is the same as seeing the real subject from 700 feet away. Due to the effect of distance, colours will appear more muted at distance and will tend to blend in together.

In modelling terms the theory is that when working in smaller scales, the paint should be toned down to appear lighter. A paint matched to an original sample as used on an actual ship will be too dark in tone for a model. This is particularly the case for the darker greys as used by Japanese warships in World War II or the Royal Navy Home Fleet. The question then is whether the paint out of a bottle is correct for the scale of the model being built.

Another consideration is that any weathering will likely darken the colour further, especially when building in 1/700 or smaller. In addition, a ship straight out of the dock and freshly painted will start to change colour almost immediately due to the effect of sun, weather, salt spray, and all the other environmental conditions that come into play. Lastly a ship will appear very different on a clear and sunny day than it will on an overcast or rainy day. These are all things to consider when deciding on the best paint match.

Quite simply, there are so many variables at play that the notion that there is only one 'accurate' paint match for a particular colour is debatable. Brighter colours such as red, blue, orange and yellow do appear on modern ships especially, and if used directly out of the bottle will be too bright and will stand out to the eye too much. Tone these colours down with some neutral grey to take the edge off the brightness; this will retain the colour, but reduce their tendency to stand out too much.

AIRBRUSHING BASICS

For most ship modellers an airbrush will achieve the best results, but it does take some practice to become confident in using it. There are some basic methods to consider that will help avoid some of the frustration of learning to use the airbrush, and which in time will lead to the modeller gaining in confidence and improving his skills. When using an airbrush there are four main variables: paint thickness, air pressure, air flow and paint volume. Trying to balance all four of these is part of the learning process, but by reducing the number of variables it can be made much easier.

Choose your paint: Whether you prefer enamels or acrylics, or you like both, find a brand you like and stick to it. All paints will behave differently; enamels are more consistently the same, while acrylics are very variable in terms of the type of thinner required, the smoothness of the paint (some can be quite grainy and regularly clog the airbrush) and its viscosity. With so many brands available it is tempting to swap around and buy whichever colour is best suited to the one required. This can become very confusing when they all work best with differing thinners, thinning ratios and airbrush pressures. By sticking to one brand you will learn how best to thin the paint and how to use it to best effect with your airbrush.

Set your air pressure to a constant value that is comfortable to use: Try to keep to this for most of your painting tasks – it should be possible to do this if the paint is thinned correctly.

Make sure the paint is thinned properly: Most of the difficulties experienced by those new to airbrushing lie in trying to use paint that is too thick. This will cause the paint to clog on the needle, and it will not atomize properly in the air flow. The response to this is often to dial up the air pressure, but this will only lead to the paint coming out of the airbrush in bursts, leading to a poor finish and a lot of wasted paint. Given that brands of paint and even colours within a range will differ in terms of thickness, it is difficult to give a ratio of paint to thinner to hold to. Instead, look to thin the paint to the same consistency as milk or ink: this means that the paint will be coloured, but will pour smoothly and cleanly without leaving a lot of residue.

Keep the airbrush clean: After each change of colour run some cleaner through the airbrush until it is clear, and give it a thorough cleaning after the end of a paint session. Remove the needle by undoing the nozzle and pulling it forwards; this prevents paint being dragged backwards through the airbrush, where it will be very difficult to clean. Clean out the cup with an old paintbrush, and use a cleaning kit brush, which can be bought for the purpose, to push through the nozzle area. Make this a regular routine at the end of each session; it is also advisable to run a little clean thinner through the airbrush before starting the next painting session to make sure it is working properly.

Keep the airbrush close to the part being painted: Around 5cm is best for decent coverage; any further away and the paint will dry before it reaches the model and cause a gritty surface.

The aim of these practices is to reduce the number of variables, because if air pressure and paint thickness are a constant and you are used to working with the paint being used, it will be much easier to manage the other variables, and more consistent and satisfying results will be achieved.

PLANNING AND PAINTING

To some extent all models need some parts painting during construction, such as aircraft cockpits, vehicle interiors, even areas of a figure that are difficult to access. As ship models are much more complex structurally than other subjects, this is more of a factor, and it requires planning out the build to a greater extent. Quite simply the aim is to progress the building of the model to the point where any further construction will make painting difficult, or will be likely to lead to damage when trying to reach tight areas. As we saw with the earlier builds of *Daring*, *Wasp* and *Nadder*, the best method is to build as much of the main hull as possible; superstructures can be included as far as possible, or built as sub-assemblies to be painted and added later. To prevent damage, the small parts are built and kept aside for painting separately, and everything is put together in the final assembly.

Priming

Regardless of the sequence chosen, the first step of any paint job is always priming. There are two purposes to priming: first and most obviously to give a base coat for the painting job, but also so that any errors can be more clearly identified, such as scratches, areas needing further sanding, or anything else that needs attention.

Primers are different to ordinary paint in that they are formulated to bond with the surface of the plastic. It is essential to use a primer when using acrylic paint, and advisable for enamels as it will result in better adhesion and a more durable finish. Acrylic primers are available, but they tend not to be as effective, nor to give as smooth a

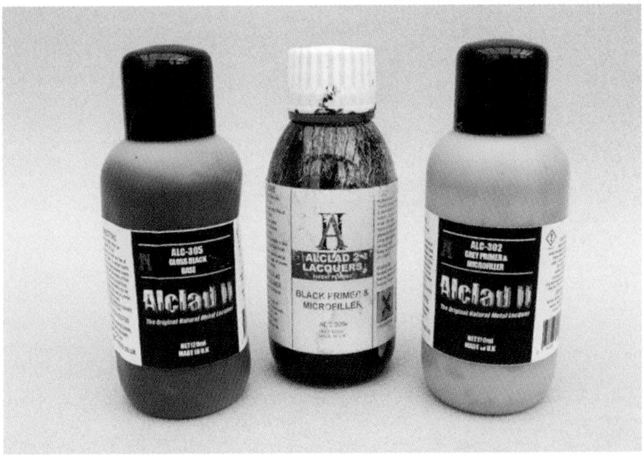

Alclad primers come in white, grey or black and give a superb finish; use a low pressure, and spray at around 5cm from the model.

The deck-edge gangways and gun tubs on Wasp *were painted before assembly and are now masked before priming.*

finish as other types. The best primer to use for all purposes is the Alclad range of primer and microfiller, a lacquer-based thinner that is already thinned for airbrush use. This gives an excellent smooth, flat surface that is ideal for small scales.

Another good option if you don't use an airbrush is the Gunze Mr Surfacer aerosols – these are available in 1,000 and 1,500 grades – or the plastic primers made for the car repair suppliers Halfords in the UK. Care is needed with any aerosol primer as there is less control over the spray so the model can easily be flooded with paint. Make sure to cover any areas that are open and have been painted earlier; a little masking tape or foam rubber from washing-up pads is very useful for this. For masking difficult areas, tape can be cut into strips to work around deck details; for round areas, such as the gun tubs on *Wasp*, a cheap punch set from car repair suppliers is ideal. Just punch out the diameter you need from the masking tape and fit it into the recess.

Painting the Main Deck

Once primed, the next decision is to paint the main deck first or last. As was said earlier, a general rule of thumb is that the more difficult and complicated the deck painting is, the earlier it should be done. In the case of a painted wooden deck, it is always best to do this first as a base colour will need to be airbrushed on before hand painting the varying tones. When using a laser-cut wooden deck there is a little more leeway, and this can be added once the main superstructure colour has been painted.

Single-colour steel or covered decks are simpler, so can be hand painted once the main colours have been finished, as with the HMS *Nadder* and HMS *Daring* builds. Use thinned paint to do this, and work carefully around the various deck detail and superstructures. If you don't have a particularly steady hand, a little masking tape around the larger areas can help to avoid mistakes. By using thinned paint, especially if you are painting with

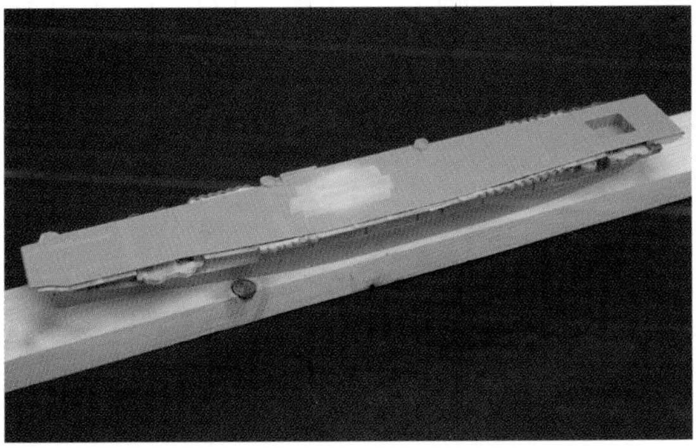

Masking before priming to ensure there is no overspray; some areas, such as hangar decks, will have to be painted as they cannot be reached later.

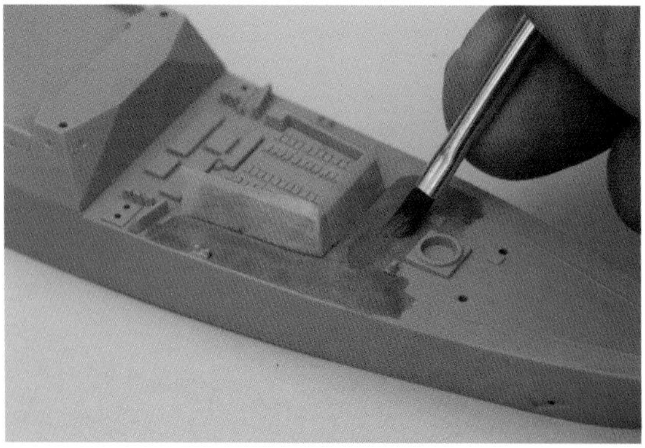

Painting decks can be one of the most difficult tasks; using a little masking, thinned paint and a flat brush will all make this easier.

acrylic, the finish will be smoother with less chance of ridges being formed by the brushstrokes.

A good tip when painting decks or platforms is to use a narrow, flat brush. This can help to get a clearer demarcation line between the deck colour and superstructure. Any mistakes can be touched up with the appropriate colour: this is one of the main reasons why the paint used needs to be good for both airbrush and hand brushing. Painting a deck does require some practice with a paintbrush, especially on a model that has a lot of deck detail; it is very easy to make mistakes and smudges, even when care is taken.

The alternative method is to airbrush the deck colour, then mask off the deck before painting the superstructure and other details. This can produce a very good paint job, but it is a time-consuming process. We will look at the technique a little later in the book, when considering the *Graf Spee* model. For those using a wooden deck, companies such as Flyhawk now often have a purpose-cut masking sheet to fit over the deck, making the task considerably easier.

PAINTING A CAMOUFLAGE SCHEME

At some point the challenge of painting a camouflage scheme will arise. These can range from simple fake bow waves, angular and geometric designs, random patterns with several colours, or dramatic dazzle schemes. Simple schemes of different coloured panels such as that worn by HMS *Nadder* are relatively easy to mask: it is just a matter of referring to the placement when applying the tape. Ships such as USS *Wasp* have a more difficult scheme to reproduce, so a little more effort is needed to get the right pattern. The main problem is getting the right shape and size of the masks; in some cases it may be easier to hand paint, and this is often the case with any camouflage pattern on the superstructure.

As always, airbrushing will give a better finish, although masking will be needed for this, as painting it freehand will result in a soft edge to the pattern, which is not correct for small-scale models. A trick that can be used to make a mask is to make a scan of the colour scheme from the kit instructions, then, using photo-editing software, crop the scan and adjust this to the same size as the model. Masking tape is then laid over the printed scan and the design is traced on to it, and then cut out; this method is used for the USS *Wasp* model.

As always with painting camouflage schemes, the lightest colour is airbrushed first since it is easier to paint dark over light than vice versa. When airbrushing over paint masks, try to angle the flow of paint at a 45-degree angle across the edge of the mask into the area that is being painted. This will help to prevent paint from being forced under the edge of the mask, and will also stop a build-up of the paint, which will cause a ridge once the tape is removed.

If the scheme requires more than one colour, continue with masking, working from lightest to darkest, until the last colour has been painted. Leave the paint to dry properly and ideally overnight before removing the mask. Do this slowly and carefully so as not to remove any of the underlying paint; this is especially important when using the more fragile acrylics.

Should there be any ridges of paint around the masks these can be removed with a very fine sanding stick, working slowly in a circular motion. If the tape is in an area that is difficult to reach, lift the edge with a wooden cocktail stick and gradually peel it back. With all the masking removed,

The masking already in place for priming is added to when painting the camouflage scheme; remember that the area to be masked is the lighter colour.

With the masking tape removed, check for any areas of overspray and touch these up. Paying attention to applying the mask well saves a lot of work later.

Masking for HMS Nadder*; the decks and platforms will be hand painted so there is no need to mask those at this stage.*

the model is then progressed through the remainder of construction before the weathering stages.

Painting Black and White Warships

Although most warship camouflages are predominantly a mix of shades and tones of grey, blue and green, the use of black or white was common for warships around the turn of the twentieth century, and for merchant ships of all periods. However, pure black and white does not look realistic on a model, as the extremes of shade are too stark for small scales; this is another result of the scale effect. A realistic white in small scales is more like off-white and yellowish in tone; some paint brands do offer something suitable, but if not, then the addition of a little tan colour will produce the desired effect.

In common with any light-coloured paint, coverage can be difficult, but using a white primer does not work well as this will serve to lighten the top coat further. The normal mid-grey primer is a

The completed painting of a white hull on the Russian gunboat Khrabry; *the colour is more realistic by being an off-white cream colour.*

better choice, and will also, of course, allow for the creation of some shade effects. It is even more important with very light colours to build up the layers gradually, as trying to cover too quickly will cause unsightly paint runs.

If anything, black is even more difficult to paint than white as it absorbs light and can result in a very flat-looking model. The dark greys used on some British and Japanese ships also produce this effect. Creating any shade around details is impossible if pure black is used, so again some change of tone and shade is needed. One option is to use a very dark grey; alternatively pure black can be toned down with a mid-grey or even some brown to create a more pleasing finish.

Painting Submarines

Submarines are a very popular choice of model, with a great deal of choice of subject and scales available. Almost all post-World War II submarines are painted black, or at least very dark grey; an overall coat of this may seem like a quick and easy way to complete a model, but it does result in something that looks rather dull. Modern submarines are generally covered in tiles to reduce the sonar signal, and the slight variation in colour of these creates an interesting patchwork effect, along with the opportunity for the modeller to create some subtlety. In fact when they have been on the surface for some time and the water has drained off them, most submarines don't appear very dark.

The Polish Navy Kilo class submarine ORP *Orzel* is produced by Bronco Models in 1/200, and is a nicely sized model of simple construction. This gives an opportunity to spend a little more time on the paintwork and sea base, the details of which are both well referenced – as with many modern vessels – by good coverage of high-resolution colour photographs found on the internet. Studying these photos, the colour of the submarine only appears very dark grey verging

Using a lighter tone for the overall colour means that black can be reserved for shading and creating depth.

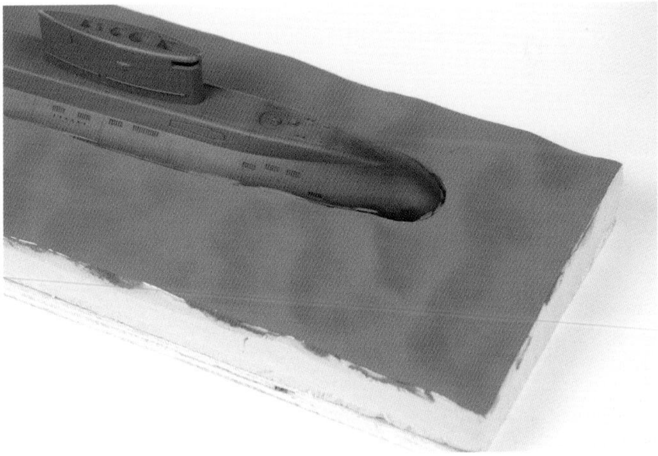

The overall colour completed and mounted on a sea base; the darker colour is retained around the bow to show areas that are still wet.

towards black around the bow and on areas that have been subject to spray; the overall colour is more of a dark brownish-grey.

Such a large model needs some work to break up the overall colour, and in this case some pre-shading to accentuate panelling visible in the photos is used. Pure black airbrushed over the main panel lines and lower hull will give some shading before the main colour is added. This is mixed using black, white and brown acrylics until the colour matches that on the photos; only then is it painted with the airbrush. Using this darker grey allows for some shading and highlighting effects, it means that details are not lost due to a very dark colour absorbing light, and it creates a more realistic look that would not be achieved if a simple overall black were used.

WEATHERING

Weathering is the process of painting the model to reflect wear, fading, rust, soot, salt streaking, and any other environmental and mechanical factor that will cause the painted steel and wooden decks from which ships are built to change. Beyond this there is painting to add depth and shade to the

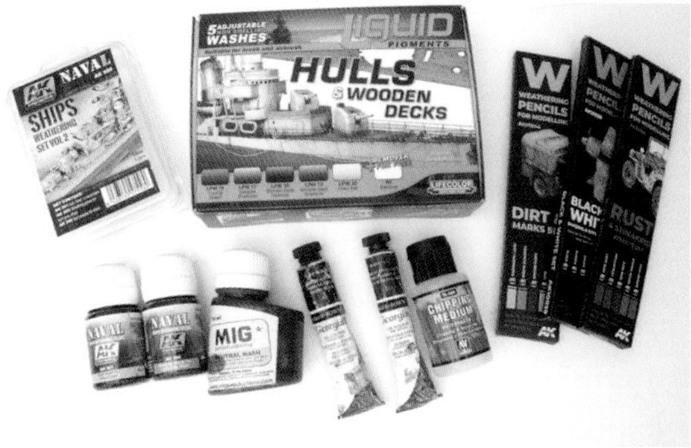

A selection of products that can be used for weathering, including a Lifecolor set specifically for ships, also artist's oils and dry pigments.

model, and to break up the monotone nature of overall greys so prevalent on warships.

As with paint, there is a huge array of products available, mainly intended for use with aircraft and armour models, with a more restricted range specifically made for ships. These products can be simply broken down into washes and pigments, although there is a lot of variety in between. In fact the majority of the products available are formulations of materials that modellers have been using for a long time, such as thinned enamel paint, oil paint and pastels, but in a more readily usable form. Of course it is still absolutely fine to keep to the basic materials, and to a large extent that is what will be used here.

Pre-Shading

Pre-shading, as used previously for ORP *Orzel*, is a technique commonly used by aircraft and particularly armour modellers to break up a single colour paint scheme and reduce the flatness of a model. It can be used on ships for the same reason, adding depth and shade, and helping to highlight horizontal areas, particularly when the base colour is very light or dark. On the HMS *Nadder* model, which has a largely white scheme, some pre-shading around the lower areas of the hull and superstructures, concentrating on areas under the platforms, is airbrushed on with a darker grey than the primer. The overall white of the scheme is then painted in thin coats to allow the grey to darken it slightly, creating a pleasing effect of shade.

Similarly white or a very light shade of grey can be used on areas such as turret tops that will catch the light, and will slightly lighten the shade of the base colour once this has been applied. There is no need to mask when pre-shading as the soft edges will help to create the desired effect. Where the model has a monotone colour scheme, and especially where there are large areas to be covered, creating a random pre-shading or

Pre-shading should not be overdone or the effect will be lost; it is used on HMS Nadder *to reduce the brightness of the light white and blue scheme.*

lightening pattern will give an effective variation to the finished model, and will mimic the uneven wear of a ship that has spent time at sea.

Sealing the Paint

The first stage of weathering, regardless of the products being used, is to seal the painted surfaces using an acrylic gloss varnish. Acrylic is used as this is more resistant to both enamel, oil and acrylic thinners: the gloss finish helps to keep the washes round the details, and prevents it spreading into the surrounding areas. Artist's acrylic varnish is ideal for this purpose, especially a good quality brand such as Winsor and Newton; this can be thinned with a little water. However, although this is fine for light weathering, it can be worn away when a lot of weathering materials are used. If that is the case, then Alclad Aqua Gloss is a good alternative; just take note of the instructions, and make sure not to shake the bottle before use.

If any decals are to be used they should be placed before weathering starts. Be careful when weathering round decals, especially hull numbers, since washes can accumulate around the edges and form an outline.

Adding Shadow

The term 'weathering' is a little misleading in that it is not entirely intended to show wear and tear:

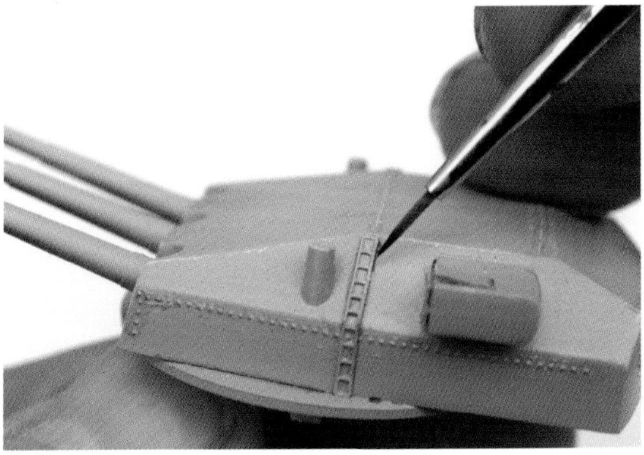

A fine brush and some oil paint is used to create shadow and depth; oil takes longer to dry, so any excess can be easily removed.

part of the process is to enhance the detail of the model by adding shadow and highlight. The first stage is to bring depth by using a thin wash to depict shadow round any raised detail. Any thinned black or dark grey paint can be used for this – aircraft panel-line washes are an option that would be ready for use, although oil or enamel paint tends to flow better and hold its colour better. For this purpose the paint needs to be the consistency of ink, as the idea is that it will flow round the object to create the effect of depth.

Using very thin paint and a fine brush, the tip of the brush need only be touched to the edge where it is needed, and capillary action will draw the paint round the object. Do this in a few places round the detail to complete it; the gloss varnish will help to pull the paint round the object and will prevent it from spreading into the surrounding paintwork. If you prefer, slightly thicker paint can be used and thin lines painted round the object; this gives a more refined look, but it does require a very steady hand. Work round the model picking out details such as doors, angles, raised areas, or anywhere where there would be a shadow or corner where light would not be as bright. Regardless of the method used, this is a time-consuming process, but one worth spending time on.

Adding Highlights

The contrasting effect to painting shadow is, of course, to do the opposite and create an impression of light falling on horizontal surfaces and edges. This is not the same as the old technique of dry brushing to lighten every raised area with a very light colour, nor is it the modulation effect employed on armour models, as both will look overdone and unrealistic in small scales. With dry brushing, every edge and angle would be lightened, whereas the aim with highlight painting is to give the impression of light falling on to a surface from a particular direction, so it is not uniformly applied. As mentioned previously, this can be done with pre-shading, and this is useful for parts of the ship that will catch the light, such

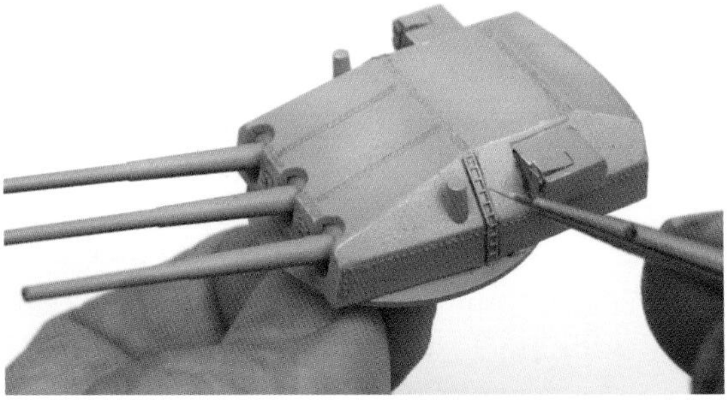

A light shade of grey, almost white, is used for highlighting; this is kept to just a few areas so as not to overdo the effect.

as the tops of turrets, deck houses and similarly flat surfaces.

Other parts that would catch the light, including any sharp angle or raised detail, can be painted with a lightened shade of the base colour and picked out with a fine brush. Consider trying to replicate the angle of the sun striking the model by using this effect sparingly, and as if light is coming from only one direction. Again this can be a time-consuming process, but gradually work over the model adding the highlights, and this will create a subtle depth to the painting that rewards the effort.

WEATHERING ON THE HULL

With the first stage completed, the true weathering stages can begin: the first step is working on the hull. Most of the weathering work will be concentrated on this area, as not only does it receive the most wear and tear, but it is also the hardest for the crew to maintain and the most difficult to reach. Some areas of the superstructure and deck will suffer from the effects of the environment and the running of the ship, but where possible these would be cleaned by the crew during time at sea and would suffer less, so weathering above the deck-line should always be done with a lighter hand.

The most important thing to consider with weathering is when to stop. Reference photographs may show the subject of your model extremely rusty and worn, but it is difficult to make this look convincing in small scales, and very easy to overdo. A better looking model will almost always result if you hold back on this stage, and only do enough to show wear without overdoing it.

Studying photos of ships subjected to a period at sea will show that the results of weathering are paint chipping, rust, salt and water streaking, exhaust stains, and movement of the crew and aircraft to be the main factors. Fouling and barnacles can be added if the model is to show any part below the waterline. Any ship in rough seas will be subjected to a great deal of wear around the bow, and this often results in the top paint being worn away to expose underlying layers or even bare metal, which will of course quickly rust. This is especially noticeable on lighter colour schemes, and recreating this is a good place to start with the weathering process.

Choose a dark grey for contrast with the main colour of the hull, and using a fine brush, work over the area of the bow around the waterline first: create a random patchwork of chips as though

Chipping around the bow of HMS Nadder *using a fine brush; keep the pattern random, but in relation to where damage to the paintwork would occur.*

Textured paint can also be used to simulate barnacles and fouling around the hull; a tinge of green is also a good addition.

the paint has been worn away. A small piece of sponge from a washing-up pad can be torn off and used as an alternative – just make sure to dab most of the paint away on a kitchen towel before applying it to the model. Larger chips can be painted around the lower bow where most wear would take place, gradually making these smaller higher up the hull. Keep this effect restrained so as not to change the hull colour completely; if you go too far, then touch it up with some of the base colour to tone it down.

For HMS *Nadder* the finished model will be shown on a rough sea base with some of the hull below the waterline exposed, so some weathering is needed here. Ships at sea for any period will become encrusted with barnacles and other marine life; this is particularly the case in tropical climates. To represent this, a suitable tan-coloured paint is applied with a stiff brush and worked around the waterline area. This can be quite roughly applied as it will help with the overall effect; keeping the paint fairly dry helps create a random pattern. Even an old worn-out brush cut down can be used for these sorts of effects with the excess paint removed.

Adding Hull Streaking

Next it is time to add some hull streaking, which helps to simulate the effects of dirty water running off the ship; it also tones down any camouflage colours and ties them together. An oil- or enamel-based paint is best for this purpose as it can be worked on for much longer than acrylics, which will dry quickly and remain fast once dried. A simple and very effective method is to use a mid-grey enamel paint, well thinned so that it is more of a coloured liquid than a paint.

Using a medium flat brush, dip this in the thinned paint and dab it against some kitchen towel so that the paint is drawn into the paper, leaving just a small amount on the brush. Now drag the brush vertically down the hull sides, and on any areas of the superstructure where streaking would occur. Do this in a random pattern so

Hull streaking showing an initial application of paint; try to vary where the paint is applied so that the end effect will not be uniform.

An old brush is used to remove most of the paint to create the streaking; dip this in thinners first, removing most of it on a paper towel.

With a camouflage scheme of lighter and darker colours, choose a colour in the middle range, otherwise the effect will be lost.

that some areas stay almost free of paint, while others have a couple of coats or more. Leave the paint for a few minutes between applications to build up layers.

Without allowing the paint to dry too much, clean the brush and dip it into some clean thinners or turpentine; the latter gives the best result, but it is strong smelling. Again, dry the brush as before so it is just moist and draw it down through the paint streaks to soften the effect, removing much of the paint in the process. Concentrate on areas where water would be expected to run off, including breakwaters; light-coloured ships will show this effect more strongly.

Adding a streaking effect on a ship carrying a camouflage scheme such as USS *Wasp* will help to soften the contrast between the different colours and produce a more in-scale and realistic finish. Choose a grey that is a middle tone to the colours you have used, as this will produce the best effect without causing any one colour to be over-emphasized. Most of the time when creating the streaking effect the brush is drawn downwards towards the waterline; in some places this can be reversed to show wear around the lower hull, but this should always be limited to just a few areas.

Adding Rust

Next in the weathering process is the addition of some rust. Any vessel at sea will quickly start to show rust stains, and if time in port is limited and maintenance not kept up, a considerable amount of rust will occur. Photos of convoy escorts in the 1940–1943 period in particular, when there was little time for turnaround in port, show extremely heavy weathering in some cases. It is tempting to try and replicate this on a model, but it is very easy to overdo it, and for some reason a very heavily weathered ship model doesn't often work well in small scales. As with all weathering, less is more, and knowing when to stop is important, as it is very easy to overdo the effect and spoil the model. For that reason oil paints are the most suitable for rust effects as their long drying time is, in this case, an advantage, since any overuse can be removed.

Rust comes in a variety of colours, but for our purposes we only really need show the staining where it has streaked due to running water, and to a lesser extent the darker areas of deep rust. Burnt sienna oil paint for streaking is a very convincing shade, and it is worth buying the more expensive artist's oils rather than student's oils as they are ground more finely and will flow better when highly thinned, which is exactly what we need.

Start by using a fine brush as before to add some chips of rust around the areas most likely to be rusty: the edges of equipment in frequent use, deck edges, and overhangs that are hard to reach

Rust is the most obvious weathering seen on ships, but needs to be restrained; use small patches and chips, never large areas.

are all good areas to concentrate on. Small flecks of the paint applied in these areas, in the same manner as the chipping applied earlier, start the process. Add some points around the deck edges, especially concentrating on areas where equipment such as boat davits, depth charges, anchor chains or anything else could be expected to remove the surface paint. Some points of rust will also occur where the paint has broken down for whatever reason: these can be added as a small dot.

The next stage is to clean the brush and dip it into some thinner, again preferably turpentine, then wipe off the excess so the brush holds only a little. Drag the paint downwards, trying to keep the run as vertical as possible, as with the streaking earlier. Here the advantage of using oil paints will be seen, because if the effect is too bold, any excess paint can be removed with the brush until it looks right.

Continue around the model, varying the length of the streaking and depth of the colour; a uniform pattern of rust all looking the same will spoil the effect we are looking for, and give too regimented a pattern. In normal conditions the paint will be workable for even a few days, so it is a good idea to take a look the next day and make any corrections. If time is a factor and you are happy with the result, drying can be speeded up with a hairdryer, used carefully.

The final step in replicating rust is to show older and more heavily rusted areas where the colour will be much darker. Any dark brown colour can be used here, and an acrylic or enamel paint can be used as we only need small areas and don't want it to run, as with the lighter shade. Pick out the centre of some of the rusted areas with the darker colour, again keeping this random so as not to overdo the effect. Combining different colours to show old and newer rust alongside runs and streaks adds a great deal of realism to the model.

WEATHERING DECKS

Along with the rest of the ship, the deck will be subject to wear from the movement of crew, aircraft or vehicles. The heaviest type of wear can be seen on aircraft carriers, although warships during peacetime, when cleaning and maintenance is more frequent, show considerably less wear and tear. On the whole it is best not to show too much deck weathering as the process will darken the original painting (or wooden deck) and can easily be overdone.

Draw the dots of oil paint downwards with a damp brush; the effect should be soft and partly blended into the surrounding paintwork.

The rust effect is completed by adding contrasting dark centres to the patches to show old and heavily rusted areas.

New Products

Painting and weathering is an area of the hobby where new products are continually being developed and marketed, as much of the focus in the model world at present is on painting and finishing. In many cases the products on offer are reworked or repackaged from the materials that have been used here, namely enamel, oil and acrylic paints, pigment powders or pastels. Learning how to use the basic materials well is the essence of producing a good model, but paying extra for the same materials already in the store cupboard might produce a quicker and easier way to create the same effects, which is of course all to the good. More often, though, it just adds another item to the modelling box, which is used only a couple of times and then forgotten about. When faced with a tempting row of new products at a model show, it is always worth thinking: do I really need it?

Deck coverings range from the traditional wooden (often but not always teak) bare or painted steel, or steel covered with a non-slip surface such as linoleum or cement-like substances. In almost all cases, with the possible exception of paint being worn away, this will cause the deck to darken as ingrained dirt becomes lodged in the surface. For our purposes this does make life a

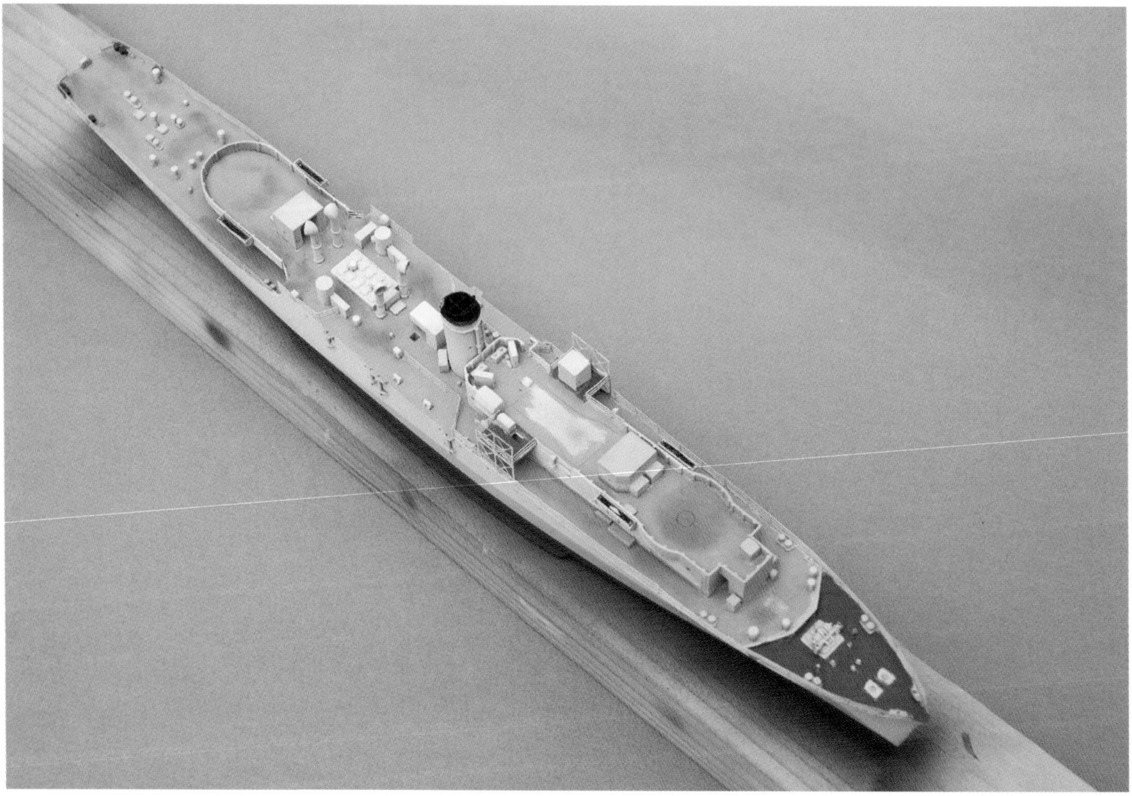

A dark grey pigment powder is used on the deck of HMS Nadder*; keeping the use restrained helps to create the subtle effect required.*

little easier, as the materials needed to create the effect are straightforward. Pastels or pigments are ideal for showing this type of wear and should be concentrated around areas of heavy use, including around weapons, boats, the bridge and walkways, and doors. Dark grey pigments can be used on any type of deck covering, although a tint towards brown is better for wooden decks.

Using a clean and dry brush, dip it into the pigment and shake off any excess, then apply it to the area where it is needed. Blow away any powder that has not adhered to the surface; a few layers may be needed to build up the required effect, but as always it is best not to overdo it. Seal the pigments with some matt varnish once completed; this usually results in the effect being reduced a little, so repeat with more pigment if necessary. Pigments allow a very soft and graduated effect to be achieved; this can be done with an airbrush, but it takes practice to get it right, and pigments are far easier.

Modern aircraft carriers provide the opportunity to depict decks that are heavily weathered: the regular movement of large and heavy aircraft and deck vehicles, combined with an extensive area open to all the elements, means that a lot of variation occurs. Fortunately modern vessels are, on the whole, well photographed, especially from above, which was rarely the case for earlier ships and all but non-existent before aircraft came into regular use. This gives an ideal opportunity to use actual photos as a reference to create a visually interesting model from what could otherwise be a rather extensive, flat patch of grey.

One advantage of using a wooden deck is that any weathering can be carried out before attaching it to the model, so saving some time spent masking, and reducing the possibility of error from paint overspray. This was the case in the build of USS *Wasp*: as an older-style carrier with a straight deck, most of the wear took place along a central line where the aircraft took off and landed. To recreate this, a thin mix of brownish grey is airbrushed along the centre line of the deck parts, progressing slowly so that the wood has a chance to dry before continuing. Too much of the thin paint could run the risk of the parts warping, so layers are built up gradually, the aim being to show discoloration rather than heavy weathering.

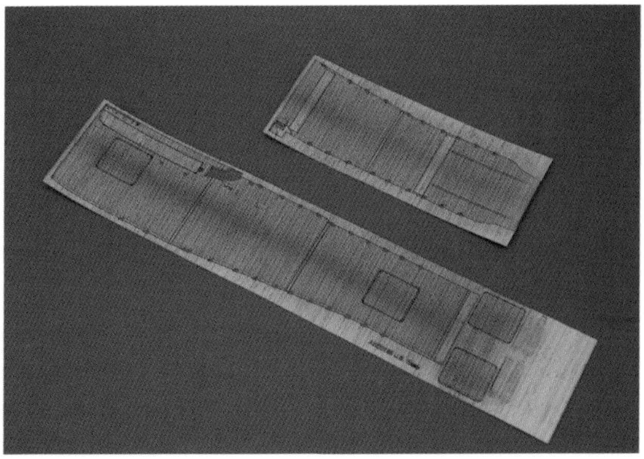

Weathering the laser-cut wooden deck of Wasp, *not forgetting the lifts. The lighter areas are where etched parts are placed.*

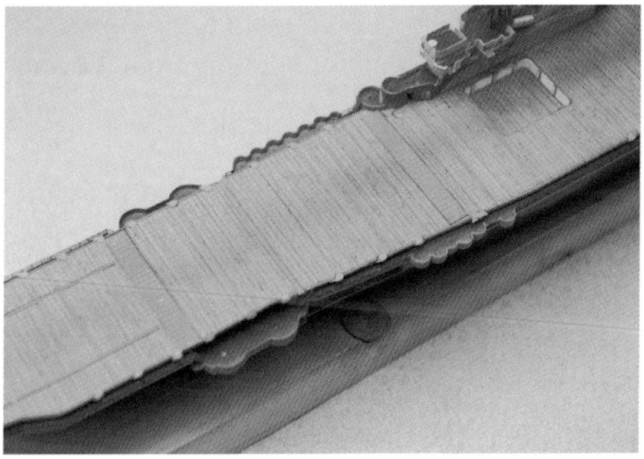

Attached to the model the weathered deck is noticeable but subtle, as intended; it shows some light wear suitable to the time period portrayed.

As a final word on the subject of weathering, always try to use original photographs as a reference for your work. This is far more reliable than taking a cue from other models, as the tendency is always to exaggerate the effect.

Chapter Eight

Masts and Rigging

Whatever your preferred type of ship model, the chances are that at some point you will need to do some rigging. This need not be an arduous task, as it almost always comes as the last part of the building stages: rigging is the finishing touch and can really bring the model to life. Fortunately these days there are a number of options for materials to make this easier, although as always a little planning and thought will be the first step.

Rigging threads from Uschi van der Rosten; these come on a spool, which is sufficient for several models and is available in standard, fine and superfine thicknesses.

CHOICE OF MATERIALS

The choice of materials for this part of the model includes stretched sprue, fishing line, wire, thread of various materials and more commonly, purpose-made rigging thread. Most important in the consideration for selection are diameter and ease of use, especially how easily it can be attached in place. For that reason and for most people, the purpose-made rigging threads such as those by Uschi van der Rosten and Infini are excellent products. Both manufacturers produce threads that have some elasticity without being capable of too much stretch: this will avoid the situation where the lines are under too much tension, causing the masts to which they are attached to bend. They also come in a variety of thicknesses so are suitable for several scales of model. Having some elasticity means that the threads do not need to be tensioned and are more resistant to damage, something very useful not only on the finished model, but during the rigging process itself.

Other than the thread, the only tools required are a good set of tweezers and a sharp scalpel; a visual aid such as an Optivisor can be useful, but be careful of using anything with too high a magnification. The higher the magnification, the shorter the depth of field – the actual distance over which an object is in focus. At high magnification, this may only be around a centimetre, so anything in front of or behind the area will be out of focus, meaning that the risk of knocking off rigging or parts already placed is increased. It is probably better to make sure that the work area is well lit and free of any draughts before reverting to the Optivisor. Most of the time the rigging material will be black, so placing a piece of white card over the usual work area will help with lighting and make the fine thread much easier to see.

The amount of rigging will vary; on modern ships, early submarines and aircraft carriers it will be very limited. Any pre-dreadnought ship would have a huge number of supports and cables, which greatly complicates the task. It isn't necessary to try and add every line unless you really want to: the impression of some rigging is often enough to add the final touch.

PREPARATION, MASTS AND SPARS

Rigging will exert a surprising amount of tension on the masts and spars of a model; if these are made of plastic or resin they can bend or break under the strain over time. Rigging a model again under such circumstances is very frustrating, and it can never be as good as the original work. The safest option then is to replace the masts with brass rod, or even better, turned brass masts that will have the correct taper from bottom to top of a real mast. Similarly, yardarms tapered at both ends are available and a great improvement over the straight rod. Masts can be cut down to the height required if too long, remembering to leave some extra height for gluing into the deck.

Should the right size not be available, a replacement can be made by selecting brass rod of the correct diameter and clamping this into the chuck of a motor tool. File down the rod on some wet-and-dry paper taped to the cutting mat until a tapered shape is achieved, being careful not to put too much pressure on the rod as it can bend.

When a limited amount of rigging is needed, it will be sufficient to use adhesives to attach the yardarms to the mast; epoxy is best for this to give a little setting time. Pay attention to ensuring that the yardarm is at exactly 90-degree angles to the mast – in fact the most important thing to consider with any mast is that it is straight and level: many an otherwise fine model has been spoilt by a wonky mast. A simple jig from plastic card cut to right angles with an engineering square is a quick solution to keeping yardarms straight whilst the adhesive sets. It can be difficult to get the yardarm exactly central, so if using brass rod, simply attach a longer length than necessary and trim to size. With a turned brass yardarm this will need to be measured out with the callipers, and the midpoint marked off.

A main mast that is not straight is very noticeable, so great care needs to be taken to make sure that it is at 90 degrees to the vertical on the length of the ship. Many masts will be slightly inclined to

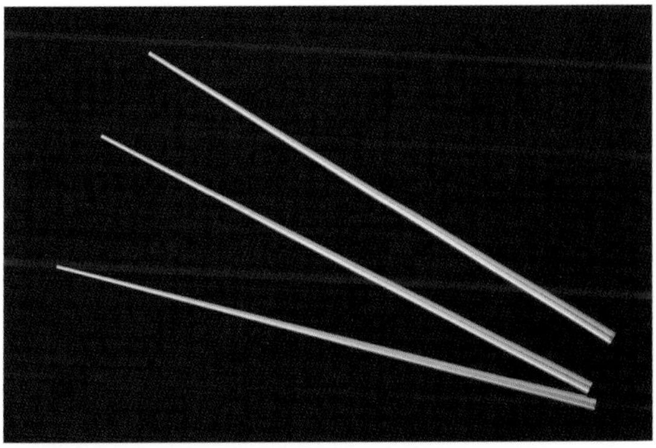

Turned brass masts and yardarms from Master Barrel of Poland come in packs with a range of sizes and dimensions, and are an ideal replacement for plastic or resin.

A jig from 60-thou plastic card is sufficient to ensure right angles are kept when constructing masts from brass rod.

stern, which adds another complication to getting it right. A home-made jig is helpful for this – aircraft modellers often use something similar for biplanes. Something as simple as Lego bricks, a piece of card with a slot cut out and some tape will suffice, as long as epoxy adhesive is used to give some time for moving the mast into the correct position before the adhesive sets. Tripod masts will have supports that are best cut from brass rod; these will not be tapered like the mast, but need to be cut to exactly the same lengths. Removing a little of the end of the rod with a metal file to give it an angle makes a neater join and also increases the area for the adhesive to grab on to.

Larger masts for 1/350 ships and above will need to be soldered to ensure that they are of sufficient strength to hold the rigging; once you feel confident with soldering this can, of course, be applied to smaller scales. Construct the main mast and yardarms first, and fix them in place before adding any supports.

RIGGING WITH THREAD

When starting out to rig a ship model it is easier to use one of the elastic threads as it is more forgiving of mistakes and knocks. If you are lucky, the kit

Soldering Masts

Soldering is a very useful skill to learn, and in larger scales it is really essential for fixing masts, as gluing will simply not form a strong enough bond. However, as the parts that need to be soldered will be very thin, only a small amount of heat from the solder iron will be required. Start by laying out the parts on a thick tile or insulating block, using a little plastic strip to raise the yardarm to the correct height, which will be the thickness of the mast it is to be soldered to. If you are using rod, then leave it over-length and trim it to size; this is easier than trying to find the midpoint. With a tapered yardarm, though, you will need to mark the centre point and make sure it is in exactly the right spot.

Once everything is in place and secure, clean up the join with a fibreglass pencil or a fine-grade sanding stick. It is also advisable to do this in the area of the join before taping down the parts.

Holding the parts down firmly on to the tile using masking tape will ensure that everything is held straight during soldering.

It is important to clean the area to be soldered as any dirt or grease on the parts will lead to a weakness that could cause the join to fail later.

you are building will have a rigging diagram, but more often it will need reference to photographs or plans to determine what is needed. Remember that it isn't necessary to add every line at first; a general impression of some rigging will suffice, and using your references you can select those lines that are most obvious. Most masts will have support stays and these are relatively easy, as are stays for yardarms; these should all be included. A ship with more than one mast will almost always have some lines or aerials running between them, so again these should be included.

At a more difficult level are the signal lines that will run from the yardarms to a point near the bridge or some other part of the main superstructure. If these are being added it is always best to start here first, since the best method is to work from inside to outside. When working with elasticated thread, measure the distance required for the line and cut a piece with about a 1cm overlap on each side to give something to hold.

To attach a rigging line, use CA adhesive and with a cocktail stick place a small dot where the line is to be placed. Lay the line on to the glue and leave it for a few seconds until it has set. Then pull the other end of the line firmly, but not too tightly, on to where the opposite end of the line is to be positioned and repeat the process. Once

The join required will only be small, and the metal to be joined is relatively thin, so a solder with a low melting point can be used, which makes the job much easier. A 145- to 188-degree solder is ideal for this purpose, and a solder flux paste will also be needed. Heat the solder iron for a few minutes until a working temperature is gained, then simply dip the tip of the solder iron into the flux paste and then on to the solder, so a small amount of both is held on the tip. Apply this to the join and it will flow round the parts, forming the join. Only a small amount will be needed, as the brass rod is quite fine; there is no need to heat up the metal at all.

After a minute the part will be sufficiently cool to remove from the tile; then clean up any excess solder with a sanding stick. Test the join by gently pushing the end of the yardarm: there should be good resistance if the soldering has been done properly. This technique can, of course, be adapted for soldering larger brass parts.

The iron only needs to be held against the join for a couple of seconds to allow the solder to flow around the parts.

When finished, a neat join results, which is not only stronger than can be achieved with glue, but also should be much cleaner.

this has fully dried, which won't take more than a few seconds, use a fresh scalpel blade to pull the excess taut, and trim this off. The line should spring back so there is no end showing from where it has been attached.

Work round the model to add lines as they are needed. For mast supports choose an attachment point where the glue spot will not show; if there is no choice then it can be touched up with a little matt varnish. Attaching to the deck or superstructure is somewhat trickier since it will not be possible to trim one end when it is against a flat surface. In this case dab one end of the line into a pool of CA before attaching it quickly in place. Elastic thread is very useful for longer runs of rigging, although it can be tricky to use in confined areas, in which case another option may be needed.

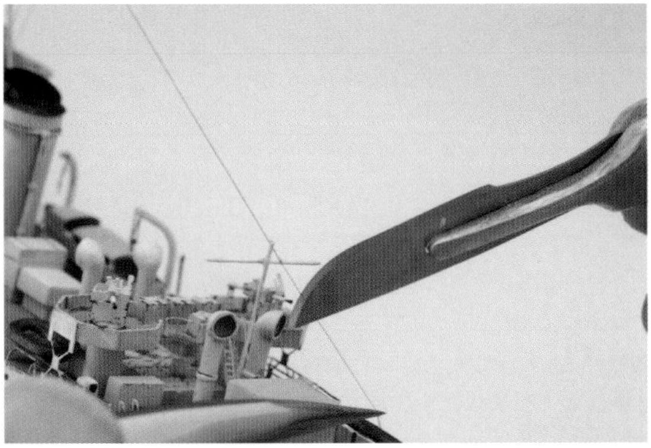

Use a fresh blade to trim the ends of the lines; pulling it taut means the blade need only be placed against the line to sever it.

Elastic rigging line is quite easy to use and has the advantage that it does not need to be tightened once in place.

Continue working around the model, finishing with any lines that run in between the masts. Be especially careful when fixing these so they are not put under too much tension, particularly if the yardarms have only been glued. After a little practice, rigging with thread becomes second nature, and as you gain confidence more complex schemes can be attempted.

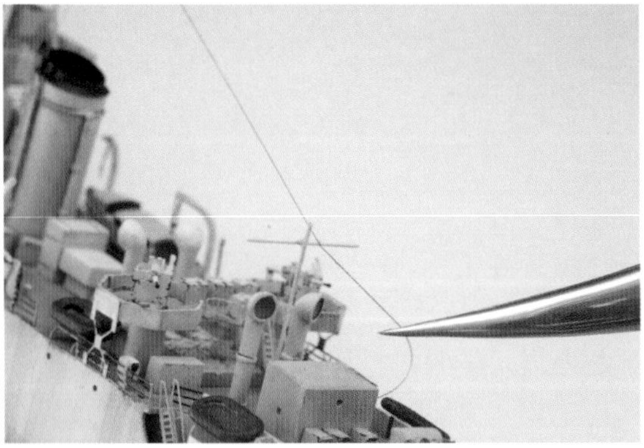

Stretch the line so there is enough tension for it to hold straight, but not too much that it will place a strain on the masts, especially when more needs to be added.

RIGGING WITH STRETCHED SPRUE

Before the arrival of elasticated threads meant for rigging models, one of the most common methods was to use stretched sprue. Unsurprisingly enough, this is simply leftover plastic sprue heated and stretched to create a thinner diameter. Of all the equipment in the modelling box, this is by far the cheapest, since it is using something that would normally be thrown away. Stretched sprue is more difficult to use for longer lines as they will have to be tensioned, although it is easier to use for short lines as it will generally stay straight. With practice it can be used for very complex rigging such as cage aerials and ratlines.

To make stretched sprue suitable for rigging, a different technique is needed. Choose a good quality plastic, usually black; all you need then is a source of heat, such as a candle, and a piece of white card so you can see the sprue once it is stretched. Cut a short length of sprue and hold one end of it over the candle flame, rotating the bottom couple of centimetres over the flame until it starts to go floppy; this will help to make a thinner and longer line.

Now lower the end into the flame so that it catches fire, blow it out after a second and quickly dab the heated end on to the card.

Unlike the traditional method of stretching sprue, only one end needs to be heated as this is the only way to get the very fine lines that we need.

With the end fastened to the card, pull back quickly to make a thin thread of sprue; if the plastic is soft enough this can extend for several feet. The sprue will cool after a few seconds, when it can be cut into shorter lengths. Repeat this a few times until you have sufficient – practise this and you will find that thicker and thinner lines can be produced, which can be used for different purposes on the model.

With the sprue ready, the process of rigging is largely similar to that for elastic thread, with the exception that polystyrene cement is used. The best for this is Revell Contacta as it is thick enough to stay in place, yet thin enough that a small dot can be dropped where needed. As the cement will quickly melt the sprue, pulling the excess off with tweezers will cause it to come away cleanly from the attachment point. Of course the cement will take longer to set than CA adhesive, so it will be necessary to progress more slowly using sprue. Should there be some excess sprue after attaching giving an untidy appearance, use a small drop of cement and carefully dab this on to the point where the sprue is attached so there is a clean break. Take care that paintwork is not damaged, however, and if necessary touch up with matt varnish.

Any longer lines of stretched sprue rigging will sag, and these can be tightened by heating. It isn't necessary to try and make the lines tight during

It is important to work quickly when the sprue has been heated; this takes a little practice, but the material costs nothing.

Extremely fine threads can be made using this method; keep the sprue from better quality kits as it will stretch more evenly.

Sprue rigging can be either cut with a scalpel blade or simply melted with a small drop of polystyrene cement.

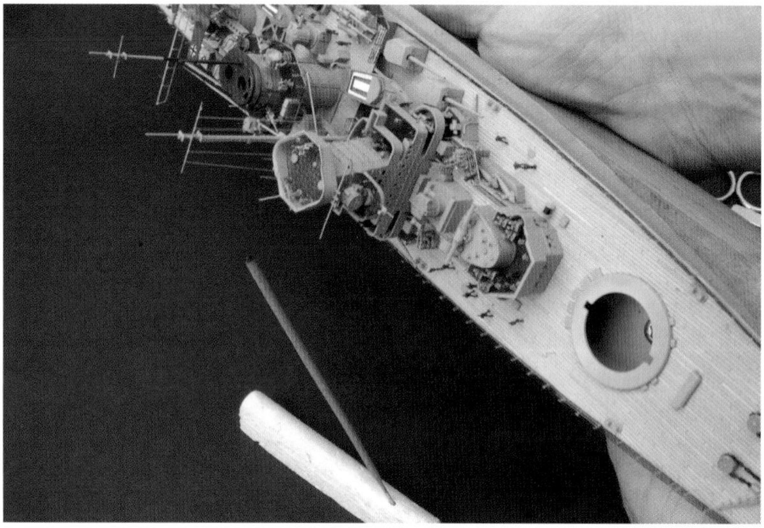

Place the incense stick into a holder so you can have both hands free to manoeuvre the model over the smoke until the rigging line snaps into place.

assembly, since any sagging can be corrected later. For that reason the focus can be on getting the line in the right position, rather than worry about it being taut. Heating the sprue will cause it to contract and tighten, although this would seem to be counter-intuitive. A source of gentle but constant heat is the most useful for this, and this is best supplied with an incense stick. These burn slowly and produce enough heat for the job, but not too much that there is any risk of melting the rigging or damaging the model, unless used carelessly. This step does require practice and a leap of faith in the results, but it does work surprisingly well.

Light the incense stick and leave it to burn for a few seconds before blowing out the flame; the stick will then continue to smoulder and produce smoke. The trick now is to allow the smoke from the stick to heat the rigging line to the point where it tightens, but obviously not so much that it will melt. Start about 10cm away from the model, and gradually bring it closer, a little at a time, until the line snaps into place. Since smoke rises, it will be necessary to hold the model at an angle or even upside down for this to work.

Needless to say, make sure that the model is securely attached to the base before starting. Tension the lines as you go, otherwise there is a risk of damaging those on the outside in trying to reach those on the inside: simply add those last and tension them at the end. Be careful as you work around the model not to get too close to those lines already completed, or they will need to be done again.

With practice, the diameter of the stretched sprue can be varied, and this is very useful to show the difference between support rigging, aerials and flag lines. Thicker sprue can be used for mast stays, and thinner for flag rigging. To give some variety, a sandy-coloured sprue can be used instead of black for signal lines, as these were often left untreated.

Regardless of the material chosen, rigging does take practice and patience to get right, but as said earlier, it isn't necessary to try and include every rigging line on the model in order to get something that creates a pleasing effect. Try different methods and see which one works for you; of course it is entirely possible to mix and match different materials on a model according to need, and as you get used to the slightly different ways of working with them.

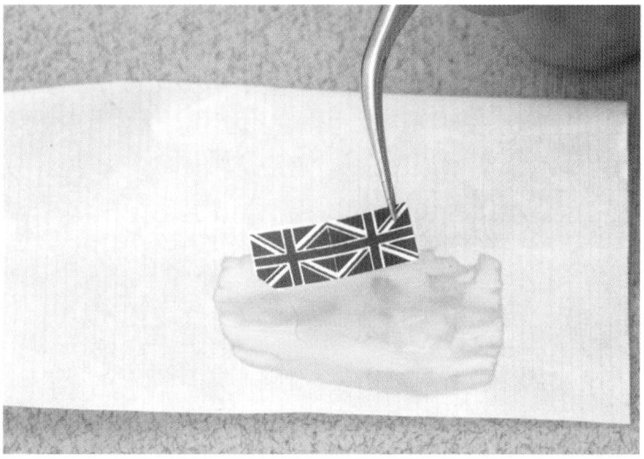

Soak the flag decal as usual in some warm water before placing it on to the cigarette paper; the PVA needs to be still wet at this point.

After it has been left to dry, trim as closely as possible round the edges of the flag so that no excess paper edges are visible.

FLAGS

Amongst all the grey of most warships, a little colour helps to catch the eye and add interest, and ensigns and signal flags are a good way to do this. These are quite straightforward to make, and almost every ship would carry them in one form or another, even submarines. Decals are one easy way, and many sheets are available for national flags, ensigns and signals of different navies and periods. Most decals will be in the form of the front and reverse printed, with the intention that it is folded back on to itself to make the finished article. Since decals are meant to be applied on to a surface, this does not always work terribly well; the decal can become stiff and brittle, and when added to the model it will stay flat, in an unrealistic manner.

To improve this we can use a piece of cigarette paper to act as a backing to the decal. First soak the decal as usual, but paint some thinned PVA glue on to the cigarette paper before applying the decal to it. Leave this to dry before cutting round the outside of the flag and folding it, with a little more PVA to finish. If preferred, the line the flag is to be attached to can be glued in place at this point, or the flag can simply be placed on to the model when all the rigging is finished. Remember that any flag would be attached to a line and not directly on to a mast or staff – a short length of thin, coloured black wire is ideal for this.

When the flag is dry, it can be crumpled a little with tweezers to give it some folds to show movement in the wind; the backing paper will help to keep the folds and will also stop the decal from cracking. Depending on the decal, you may need to finish off the flag with a little matt varnish, as some can be quite glossy.

The flag can be folded round the rigging line it is to be attached to; a thicker line of stretched sprue or thin wire is best for this, as it will need to be rigid.

Although cigarette paper is very fine, once folded with the decal on each side the result can be rather thicker than is desirable. To improve on this it can instead be painted on to the paper so a very thin flag results. As the flag will be crumpled it isn't necessary to have too much detail, especially in 1/700; we only really need to give the impression of the actual design and colour. Use a water-based paint – acrylic or poster paint is ideal – and paint the design on both sides of the cigarette paper; it is thin enough so that once one side has dried it can be turned over and the design will show through.

Let it dry, then cut it out and attach it as previously. Again, crumple the flag with tweezers – any lack of detail on the flag itself will not be noticed, but it will be thin and closer to scale. Any number of flags can be added using these methods; just check that you have them in the correct location, and refer to photographs to check when national flags and ensigns are flown: this usually varies between the navies of different countries.

There is no need to be neat when painting the flag design on to cigarette paper, as the edges will be trimmed to tidy it up later.

Cut the flag down, taking care to retain the correct dimensions; then it can be made to look as though it is blowing in the wind by adding folds.

Chapter Nine

Water Bases

WHY WATERLINE?

As ship modellers we have the opportunity to show a finished model in its natural element, the water. Of course the traditional way of building a ship model as a full-hulled museum-type piece is popular with many, and rightly so. Personally I find the challenge of replicating water in all its variety a fascinating one, as it allows some freedom for artistic impression, and of course brings the possibility of creating the story-telling element of dioramas, which can't be done with the full-hulled museum style. Of course there is always the chance of getting this part of the build wrong and detracting from an otherwise excellent model, but by following a few simple principles, and starting with easy seascapes to learn some of the techniques, a convincing and attractive water effect can be produced that will greatly enhance the final impression.

Most 1/700 kits will be in waterline form; with 1/350 there is more choice as the majority will be full hull, so can be cut down if required. Having the option to leave a little of the lower hull is good for showing the model in a heavy sea, since some of the lower hull would show as the ship pitches and rolls. This can always be added to an otherwise waterline model with a little plastic card if the same effect is required. Some dramatic and exciting models can be produced with a well-made sea base, from harbour scenes, ships in action, stormy weather or even ultimately sunken. Learning to make an effective sea base allows for an almost endless possibility for naval and civil scenes and dioramas.

This model of Gdynia harbour in Poland on the eve of World War II shows that there are plenty of subjects to create when using a water base.

WATER COLOUR, WAVES AND WAKES

Quite often attempts to make a sea base fall into the trap of making some basic, common mistakes, which seem to be repeated over and over again. Possibly this is the result of modellers using other models as reference, rather than photographs of ships at sea. Given the number of excellent ship photographs available in reference books and on the internet, it is very easy to spend a little time looking at these photos to see exactly how water looks when a vessel is moving through it. This is really the starting point in learning how to make a realistic sea for your model, and it is worth spending some time doing this.

Water Colour

It will quickly become apparent that one of the most common mistakes is using an overall colour, which is not realistic. The actual colour that water appears will vary greatly according to weather, depth and location. In bright sunlight the reflected light from the surface will make it look brighter, while on darker days, the opposite will apply. Coastal waters being shallower can be lighter in colour, although this will vary greatly according to location, as rivers carrying silt or even pollution will tend towards a brown hue.

Regarding location, consider where your model is to be set, and try to find some reference photos. It is a generalization that tends to hold true that Pacific waters are bluer than Atlantic, which tend more towards grey and green. The most common mistake, however, is to use too bright a blue, which is fine for a Pacific coral atoll but not for the mid-Atlantic Ocean. It is safer to tend towards darker blues and grey/greens, which will also help to provide contrast to the model. Having said that, a bright blue sky will make the sea look much lighter in a photograph, but this is difficult to replicate in model form since the area of the base will almost always be quite small. The smaller size means the colour appears exaggerated since it is concentrated in a limited area, and it is then difficult to create the right effect without making this look far too bright.

Making Waves

Another common error is to make waves in parallel lines, as they look when coming into the coast, where most of us would tend to see the sea. This doesn't really happen away from the coast, so avoid replicating this on the model base as it looks odd. Again, look at photos for reference and see how waves in calm seas are much more regular in size and distribution, but as it becomes rougher they vary in height and spacing. Avoid using too much bright white for rougher seas – this can easily be overdone.

Wake Patterns

Wake patterns are quite a technical matter, and depend on the hull shape of the ship, its speed, and the sea state. General principles will apply, as the physics of a body moving in water are constant and for our purposes can be reduced to a relatively simple form. A ship moving in water will create two types of wake that we can try to replicate. The first is a turbulent wake, which is the area of white water immediately surrounding the hull. This is quite narrow and does not extend much beyond the same width, regardless of length. The second is the Kelvin wake, which

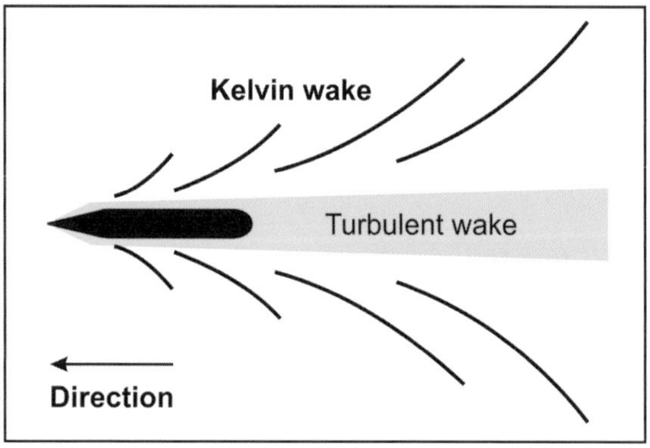

A simplified diagram showing the pattern of wake made by a ship in most sea conditions and at a range of speeds.

is a regularly spaced, curving crest of water that spreads around 20 degrees from the centreline of the hull.

Reference to photographs will show this principle to be the case, yet many models are presented showing a bow wave coming off at an unrealistic angle, something we have all no doubt done at one time or another. If you are unsure, consider whether the end of the wake is where it could be from where the bow is breaking the surface, and you will not go far wrong.

CHOICE OF MATERIALS

The list of materials that have been used to make a sea base is long and at times quite bizarre. Mostly this stems from the fact that unlike the seemingly endless products available for military, aircraft or railway modellers, ship modelling has been somewhat neglected in terms of what could be termed the scenery. Starting from the simplest, as used previously for the HMS *Daring* build earlier in this book, a range of foamboard bases with photographic prints are available from Coastal Kits, which give a very quick solution to the problem. These come in a range of sizes and look very good, although of course they are completely flat and without any three-dimensional effect.

Of the materials that are available, most are variations on the theme of artist's acrylic gel, either clear or coloured, or thick and thin formulations. This is a water-soluble paste that is meant for thickening acrylic paint to produce a similar finish to oil paints; it dries almost clear, and is very useful for creating wave and wake effects. My personal preference is to use this in combination with a thick foamboard base and heavy watercolour paper, as this gives the flexibility to create bases ranging from dead calm to very rough. It is also relatively inexpensive and can be used for a variety of scales and sizes.

Some other materials that will be needed on occasion include PVA glue, toilet paper, artist's gesso (a type of primer for canvas), gloss varnish, and of course paint. Since the area to be painted may be quite large, it is uneconomic to use more expensive modelling paint for the sea base. Craft acrylics are fine for this purpose and much cheaper; they come in a wide range of colours, with the darker blues and greens being especially useful, along with black and white and some lighter greens and turquoise for the wake. For very bright highlights, products intended to create snow effects, such as Vallejo Foam & Snow, are very useful as they are a thick type of paint that retains a pure white colour very well, but these need to be used sparingly.

Foamboard bases from Coastal Kits are a cheap and simple way of displaying your waterline models effectively.

Acrylic gels and other materials used for making the water base; most of these can be found at a good art shop.

With so much emphasis on painting and finishing models at the moment, new products are being developed all the time, which may help to create the effects we are looking for. But choosing the easily found materials described above and using them well is the basis for this element of the model.

Clear resin is often used by modellers to represent the sea, and this can look good when done well. However, it does have several disadvantages, namely cost, difficulty of handling, smell and drying time. For these reasons it is not a material I like to use, and it will not be covered here; by all means experiment with it, but care must be taken, and be sure to follow the instructions for use to get the best results.

MAKING THE BASE

Regarding the base, the first thing to do is to work out its dimensions. The length of the model will be the most important factor, but there needs to be some space in front and behind the hull to give some room to create the wake effect. Shortening the front and rear of the model too much will make it look cramped; this also applies to the width of the base, as making this too narrow will limit the area we can use to create the wake and the appearance of movement. If you intend to provide the model with a case, then fit the proportions of the base to it; having a case specially built to the dimensions of the completed model is likely to be much more expensive.

With the dimensions worked out, a piece of thick insulating foam is used for the main part of the base. This can be bought in metre-long pieces or more and cut to size carefully with a sharp knife. If a case is to be used, then plywood cut to a slightly larger size to allow it to sit over the model is sufficient, although better quality wood will improve the finish. The early stages of the base need to be completed very early in the build, ideally before anything other than cleaning up the hull.

First the direction of the model and its placement is worked out; then draw around the hull to mark its exact location on the foamboard, which can then be cut out. It always looks best to place the ship at a slight angle on the base: this gives it more visual appeal than if it is parallel to the edges. Test fit the hull into the base, making any adjustments to the size of the cutout as necessary. Any gaps can be easily filled, but try not to make these too large as it will then be difficult to set the model firmly in the base.

Creating the Wave Pattern

The wave pattern can now be formed by pressing into the foamboard: it is soft enough so that impressions can be made easily, but firm enough to hold them. A suitable tool will surely be found around the house – anything with a rounded end is ideal, such as a ball-pein hammer, a screwdriver, a file, or anything that can be pushed firmly without risking damage to the hand.

How much of a wave pattern is needed will depend on the sea state the model is to be shown in; a fairly calm sea needs only have the flat surface of the foamboard. It doesn't matter at this stage that the surface of the foam is rough, as this will be smoothed out in the next step. Try to avoid

Foamboard as the basis for the sea is light, easy to work and readily available from DIY shops; this is the base used for the USS Wasp *build.*

making the waves in a rough sea too uniform, because as the sea state increases in roughness, so the height and distribution of the waves becomes more varied; the best reference for this is, of course, photographs.

Creating the Surface of the Sea Base

Next we need to use watercolour paper to create the surface of the sea base. Cut this oversize to the foamboard by a couple of centimetres and soak it in water for five minutes to make it more pliable. Drain the paper and quickly pat it dry before sticking it down on to the foamboard using UHU Por glue, which is formulated for use with foam. Other types of adhesive will simply cause the foamboard to dissolve, and PVA does not give a strong enough bond to allow the paper to conform to the curves of the waves.

Apply the glue to the foamboard, working quickly as it starts to set in a few minutes; then use a cloth to push the watercolour paper on to the foamboard so that it touches the surface. With the paper still damp it is much easier to push it into contact with the lower areas; you may need to hold it in place for a short time. Leave it to dry for a few hours until the paper is stiff once more.

Cutting out the Recess for the Hull

Now cut out the recess made for the ship's hull by placing the hull bottom on the paper at the desired angle and drawing round it. The value of doing this early on in the model build becomes apparent, since to do so with the built model would risk a much greater degree of damage. The edges of the foamboard will be rough, but these can be finished off by gluing plastic card, balsa wood or any other thin and easily workable material around the edges.

Balsa has been used for the builds in this book because although it is not very resistant to knocks, this won't matter a great deal since the completed models will be in a case and therefore protected. Again using UHO Por, 5mm balsa strips are glued to the outside of the base, and any gaps filled and sanded. A nice undulating edge to match the surface of the water can be carved before the wood is sealed ready for painting.

Painting the Base

With the basics of the base finished off and the edges tidied up, we are ready to start painting. Choose your colour, bearing in mind the location your model is to be shown in, and give the watercolour paper a few coats of this to create a solid base colour. If this colour is a mix rather than out

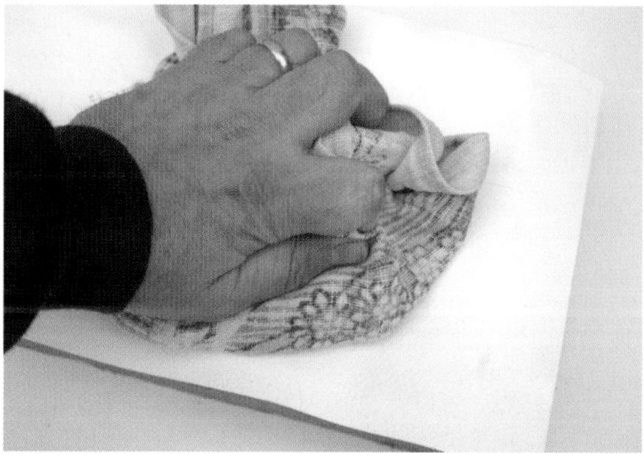

Pressing the watercolour paper down on to the foamboard will smooth out any rough edges made when creating the waves.

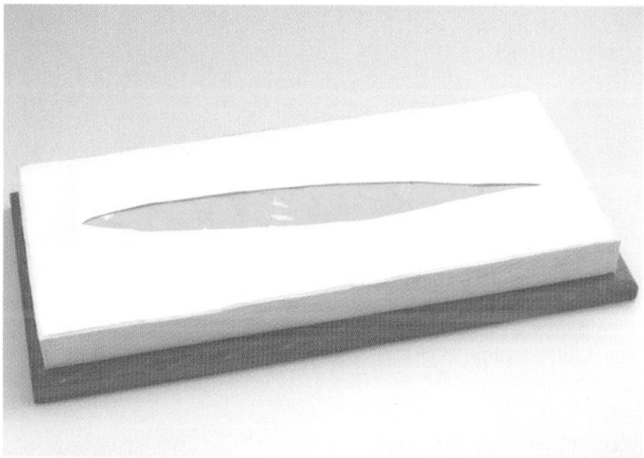

Once the paper has dried it can be trimmed with a sharp knife, and the base then neatened up by adding some edging.

Use a wide brush to build up the base colour on the watercolour paper with acrylic paint; at this stage we are just looking for a solid colour.

of the bottle, be sure to make plenty and keep it in a sealed jar as we will need more of it for the next stages and for touching up later.

Next some lighter blues and greens are airbrushed on to show the higher points of the waves where the colour is lighter. Due to the darker background, this will need to be gradually built up; this gives the opportunity to grade the colour so that it is more solid at the tips of the waves. If you overdo the lighter shades and the base colour starts to change too much, go back to the reserved base shade and airbrush this over the areas that are too light.

Quite often the surface of the watercolour paper will provide a good enough wave pattern, but if something a little more pronounced is required, then acrylic gel can be applied for a slightly rougher surface. A medium-sized flat brush used in a stippling motion is used to apply the gel, slowly working over the surface in small areas at a time. Try to keep this as uniform as possible, or it is likely that the last area covered could be quite different to the first.

Securing the Hull to the Base

With this first stage finished, the base can now be set aside until the model is mostly completed, or until you reach a stage where you feel comfortable in attaching it. This all really depends on the individual model; it may be easier to have something to hold on to whilst progress continues, although a large base can be difficult and heavy to manoeuvre. Too late in the build and there is the risk of damaging any masts or similarly fragile parts whilst working on the seascape. In the case of USS *Wasp*, this was left until the model was almost completed, since it was easy to work around because it doesn't have much in the way of masts and rigging.

The hull bottom is glued to the base with epoxy or UHU Por if it is going directly on to the foam. In

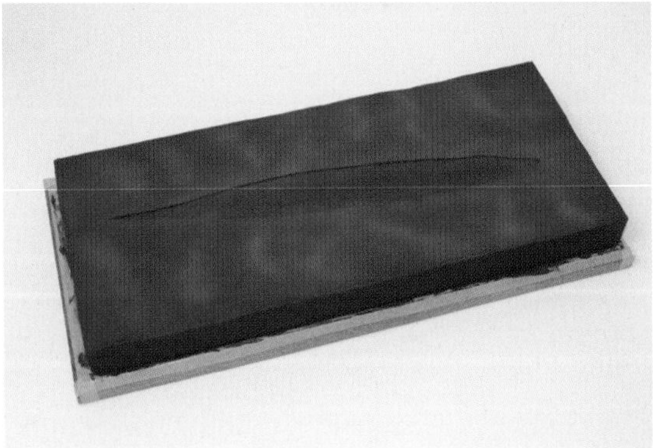

Lighter tones are kept quite restrained so that the overall base colour is not altered too much.

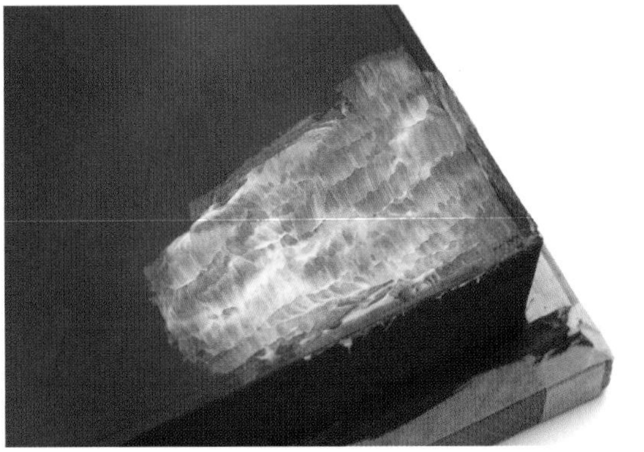

The layer of acrylic gel will also help to blend the base and highlight colours together, since it dries slightly opaque in thicker layers.

Any peaks left can be softened out by going over them lightly with a wet brush before the acrylic gel fully dries.

cases when the model itself is heavy, such as those with a solid resin hull, it may be advisable to drill through the base and screw the model down using self-tapping screws. This has the extra benefit of preventing the hull from warping, which resin can do, especially when stored in a very warm room.

Creating the Wake

Once the hull is secured in place and the adhesive has been left to dry for at least twenty-four hours, work on the sea base continues with the creation of the wake. Acrylic gel is used to build up the shape of the wake, remembering the earlier diagram as to how this should look. The first step in this process is to seal any gaps between the hull and the base.

To show the disturbed water of the wake, some thinned, light green craft acrylic paint is used; this is actually more like a wash, as the paint is very thin so it will settle into the recesses formed by the gel. A few coats will be needed to build up the colour, but continue to keep the paint very thin at this stage.

A ship moving at any speed that is more than dead ahead will create some form of bow wave, along with breaking waves at the edge of the wake. If the model is to be shown moving at a slow speed, then this can be made simply with acrylic gel, which will hold a soft peak sufficient to show a small wave. Anything more substantial needs more work, as using only gel will result in a solid-looking wave, when really we are looking for something that is lighter and airier in appearance. A couple of methods can be used; one of these will follow later as it is used for making rough water and for submarines.

For the *Wasp* model, toilet tissue is used to build up layers in the wake gradually, with the help of PVA and CA adhesive. Tear off some oversize pieces of paper, and using slightly thinned PVA, work this into the area of the bow wave and leave to dry. Using tweezers, pull away the excess paper, leaving a ragged edge, then apply some CA adhesive to the edge of the paper; this will harden it

Acrylic gel brushed on the base to create the wake; once dried, the gel will lose most of its white colour and will also shrink slightly.

The wake round the hull of the ship is disturbed water, which will be a lighter colour.

Bathroom tissue is the most suitable for making light water effects as it has no pattern, dissolves easily, but can be built up in layers.

Build up the layers of paper until sufficient depth is achieved; using CA adhesive on the paper also means that it is stiff and can be bent into shape.

and cause it to go clearer. By building up layers of paper in this way, a more open effect results, while painting white just around the edges of the waves adds to the effect by creating the impression of the wave breaking.

Breaking Waves

The same technique can be used to show breaking waves in other areas of the base. Small areas are first painted white, so as to show through the paper. Smaller pieces of toilet paper are then pushed into place using a brush and thinned PVA; as they start to break up they can be blended into the base to give an effect of breaking water, which is very convincing once painted. Keep this restrained, as too much white in the wake can look as if the model is on a bed of toothpaste; the edges of the wake and some waves within it are enough to create the sensation of movement.

The stern is an area where more rough water will be found due to the propellers, so a little more gel and white paint can be added there to create the effect. Paint products meant to simulate snow such as Vallejo Foam & Snow can be used, since this gives a very bright white. However, this is best used sparingly along the tips of breaking waves to achieve a highlighting effect. It is easy to overdo these effects, so if in doubt touch up with a little more of the base colour, or the green used for the wake, to tone the white down a little. Too much white in this part of the model is a common

The finished wake on the USS Wasp *model; resist the temptation to add too much white, as less will make it more realistic.*

mistake, so follow that wise adage in modelling: when you think just a little more will do it, stop.

Gloss Varnish to Finish

With the base painting finished, several coats of gloss varnish can be painted overall to give as much shine on the water as possible. Any varnish with a high shine is suitable for this, although oil-based varnishes have a tendency to yellow over time, so these are best avoided; something with a quick drying time is ideal, as a few coats will be needed to build up the full effect. Carefully polishing the dried surface with a soft cloth can help to add that last little bit of gloss.

A sample of watercolour paper airbrushed in one direction with blue paint to show how the texture of the paper produces a wave effect.

CALM WATER

It isn't always necessary to show a ship in motion or on the open sea: a harbour scene or a ship at anchor can make for a very interesting model, especially when smaller craft such as tugs and barges are included. Calm water is, of course, the simplest type of sea base and needs only watercolour paper, paint and varnish, with perhaps a little acrylic gel to seal any areas around the hull where it meets the paper. Here the texture of the paper can be used to good advantage by using thinned paint and the airbrush set to around 10psi.

Hold the airbrush at a low angle to the paper and gently spray across the surface; the ridges in the paper will pick up the paint and leave a shadow behind it. A very pleasing effect can be achieved if the darker base colour is painted first, then highlighted in this way; a silvery grey to mimic sunlight on the water is a good choice for the highlight colour, otherwise lighter shades of green and blue used very sparingly will result in a two-toned effect. As before, everything is finished off with a gloss varnish.

Remember that for a harbour scene, the water is more disturbed and quite often dirty, laden with silt or even polluted, so the colour will tend much more towards browner shades than in the open sea.

This model of the Russian gunboat Khrabry *is shown at anchor on a simple, calm sea base, which is easy and effective.*

ROUGH WATER

Modelling rougher water is more challenging, but by modifying and adding to the basic method that we have already, a dramatic scene can be created. Full-hull models are suitable for rough-water scenes since part of the hull will need to be shown, either the bow rising out of the water, or below the waterline as the ship rolls. If the model is waterline, a little planning and some strips of plastic can serve to show part of the hull.

Making the Base

As before, insulating foam is used for the base, but this time it is a thicker section to give more depth for carving deeper waves. As previously, the hull position is marked out first, and then cut out using a sharp knife; when the foam is thick it may be easier to cut out the hole completely rather than trying to gouge out the excess foam. Waves are now formed using a knife and by pushing them into place, following the same process with the use of watercolour paper as previously.

Paint the base with the chosen colour as before; with a rougher sea more shading and highlighting is needed to emphasize the difference between the troughs and crests of the waves. First a darker shade of the base colour is airbrushed into the lowest areas of the base in between the waves; this is then contrasted with the colour of the crests of the waves, which are highlighted in light green.

Choose a direction from which to airbrush a lighter blue: this mimics the effect of sunlight coming from one direction; this is then sprayed on one side of the crests of the waves, as previously. It may seem unnecessary to show light on what may be intended as a base showing a ship in stormy weather, but this will help to create contrast and texture on the water.

Airbrushing a dark shade of the base colour into the troughs will increase the effect of depth when contrasted with highlights.

A lighter blue than the base colour brings the effect of light into play by giving the impression of the angle the sun is striking the model.

Making the waves for a rough base; it is best to sketch out the position of the crests of the waves before starting to carve.

With a thinned light blue colour, the tips of the waves are painted to show where the water is breaking. Start by painting over the area with water; then working from the crest downwards, blend increasingly thinned paint into the lower parts of the wave. Make sure to keep the area wet and the paint thin; it should be almost like coloured water, and must be allowed to dry before building up the effect. If the colours from the last stages are too bright, or there is too much contrast, it can be toned down by airbrushing a thin coat or two of the base colour over the whole.

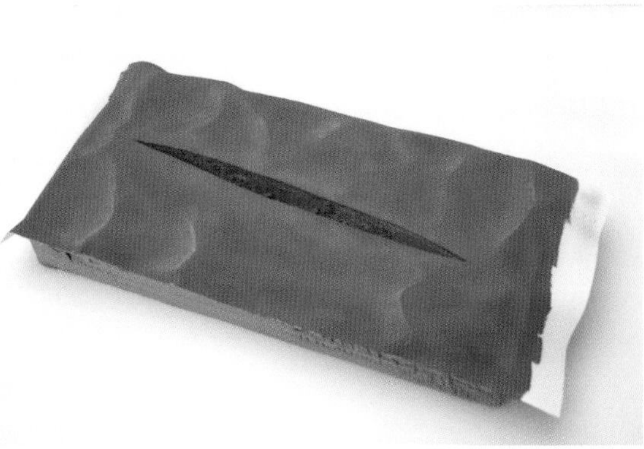

Choose a light blue colour for this stage of painting as the effect needs to be subtle, but still bright enough to show through after further painting.

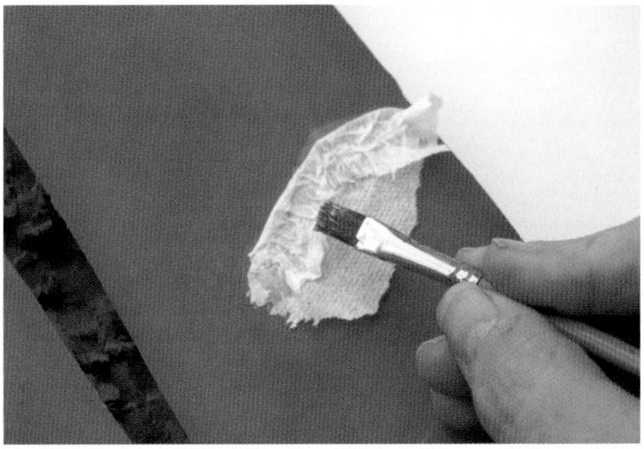

A flat brush will help to push the paper into smaller waves; it needs to be quite stiff to help break up the paper.

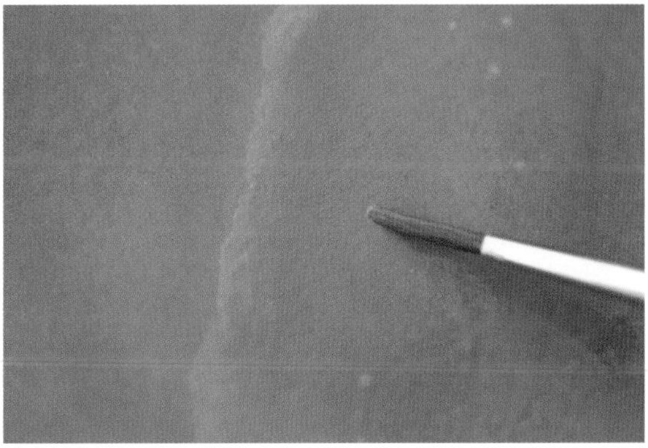

It is important to keep the area wet when using acrylic paints for blending; this is a technique commonly used by figure painters to create folds in clothing.

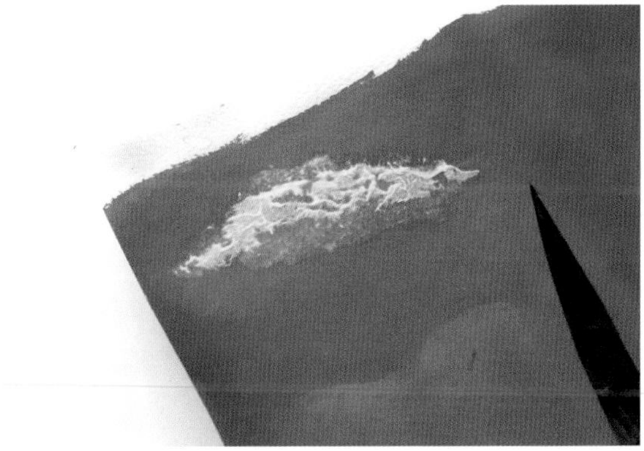

Using toilet paper gives more of a three-dimensional look to the water, rather than just using paint to try to create the effect.

Making the Crests of the Waves

In rough weather the crests of the waves will break and create foam: this effect is made, as previously, from toilet paper and PVA glue. Using a flat brush, place a line of the PVA along the crest of the wave and allow the paper to dissolve into it. Push the paper into a suitable shape to represent the breaking water, using more PVA. Don't thin the glue too much, though, as the process can become quite messy; it needs just a little water for this to work best. Vary the amount of broken water shown on each wave so that it doesn't look too uniform.

Once the paper has dried thoroughly, paint the tips of the crests of the waves with a pure white paint to highlight the areas of breaking water. Extend this down the face of the wave to show how the wind creates foam around where the wave breaks.

With this finished, the main part of the base is now completed and we can place the model into position and begin to blend it into the scene.

Water and Wave Effects around the Model

Positioning a full-hull model into the base allows an opportunity to show a little more motion in

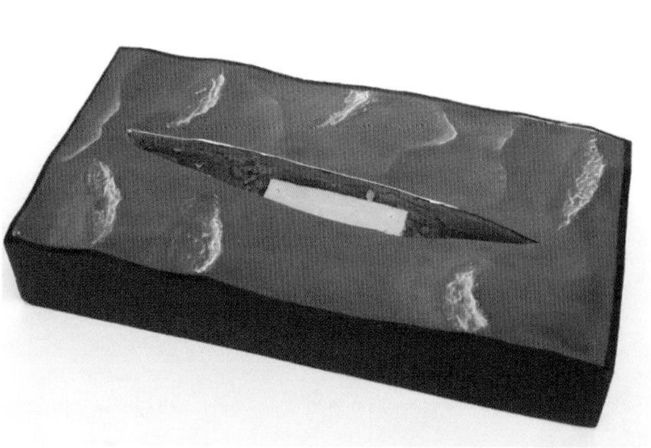

The base completed and ready for the model; the gloss coat to finish will cover any marks left by the PVA or painting process.

Cotton wool placed around both sides of the bow; if the strands are not damped down it can be seen how they will look unrealistic.

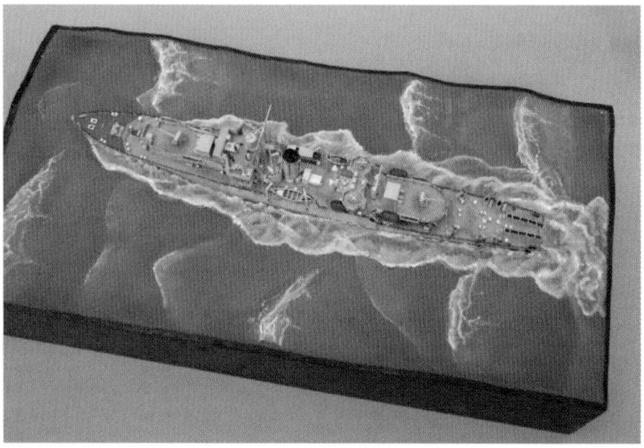

In a similar way to the breaking waves, the edges of the wake are made by pushing the small sections into place, this time using acrylic gel.

the ship than perhaps with a waterline subject, as the natural pitch and roll of a ship in heavy seas can be much more easily shown. In this case the HMS *Nadder* model is shown ploughing through a heavy swell, with the bow rising and something of a roll to port. Once the model is in place the wake is made as before using acrylic gel and a combination of lighter greens and blues to indicate the disturbed water.

A different technique is needed when it comes to showing bow and stern waves in rougher water, since we need to try to create an impression of spray and foam. Many modellers use cotton wool for this and it is a good choice, but it does need some treatment to get the best out of the material. One of the main problems with cotton wool is that it is formed of fibres that tend to separate and especially close up, which spoils the effect. It is also matt, and although foaming water does not reflect light as much as still water, it nevertheless does need some help to prevent it contrasting too much with the otherwise glossy surface of the sea base.

To use cotton wool, first dab some PVA on to the area around the bow, then pull off a piece of cotton wool and push this into position. Once dried, pull away some of the excess with tweezers until it is about the size needed.

To get the effect of flowing water, the cotton wool is treated with acrylic gesso: this is intended for use when preparing an artist's canvas for acrylic paint, but it dries hard and retains its whiteness, which is very useful for our purpose. Using a flat brush, the trick is to dab small amounts of the gesso on to the cotton wool and draw the brush backwards and downwards. The gesso will stay on the surface of the cotton wool and draw the fibres together, creating a stream effect. Any stray fibres can be brought in with the gesso so that a wave effect is created.

At the edges of the wave, use more gesso to blend the cotton wool into the surrounding area, so creating the effect of the bow wave running into the wake. Add smaller amounts of cotton

With the cotton wool treated with acrylic gesso, tease the wave into shape using tweezers until it creates the look you want.

Adding some extra water that is draining off the hull is a realistic addition when showing a ship in heavy seas.

wool to extend the rear and edges if a little more is needed to blend into the surrounding water. Similarly for the stern wake: this method can be used to create a little foam around the propellers.

In heavy seas water will fall and accumulate on deck, and of course this will run off at some point. Water on deck is simply added with gel and a little gloss varnish, while water draining off the deck is just a matter of altering the cotton-wool method slightly. The gel needs to be pooled around areas such as the breakwater and any other drainage holes, depending on how much flow you want to represent.

For the water draining off the deck, pick off and slightly flatten a small piece of cotton wool, and trim one end with scissors to make it easier to attach the end of the breakwater is a good place to position this. With a little gel, attach the cotton wool in place and arrange it into a suitable position to show water flowing from the deck. As before, a little gesso will tidy up any stray fibres and give a sensation of flow and movement to the water; a little more will help it blend into the rest of the wake.

WATER BASES FOR SUBMARINES

Because modern submarines are of a largely similar shape, they tend to produce a distinctive and consistent type of wake. Rather than a bow wave, the water is forced over the forward part of the hull, and the wave forms behind a trough created by the pressure of the water being forced upwards. The model of the Polish Kilo class submarine ORP *Orzel* ('eagle' in Polish) is a good example of this, and the method used for the sea base for this model could be applied to any modern or indeed earlier submarine with a similar hull shape.

With the model mounted on the base, layers of acrylic gel are built up around the bow to create the effect of water being pushed over the rounded hull. This needs to be kept smooth: working with a wet spatula is a good way to achieve this. The area just behind the bow is pushed down a little further, making use of the foam base to do this. Immediately behind this more gel is used to start to build up the breaking wave caused by the movement of water.

Once again the disturbed water and breaking waves are made from cotton wool and gesso, with the exception that this time a lighter effect around the stern is needed. A smaller amount of cotton wool is glued in place, then teased out with tweezers to create an open, cloud-like effect. Gesso applied lightly over this hardens enough to hold it in position, and creates some very nice patterns over the surface.

Making the Wake

For this model of the *Orzel* the wake is made in a different way. Photographs show the wake

Submarines create a different wake pattern to normal surface ships, and methods need to be adapted a little to create the right effect.

By teasing out the fibres of the cotton wool a very light and airy effect can be achieved once gesso is painted over to harden off the surface.

pattern to be made up of lots of small, foaming waves, so a different material and technique is used to try to match the look in the photos. A product from Mig Ammo, Acrylic Water 'Wild River Waters', was used for the first time as an experiment. This is a viscous, gel-like substance, slightly pink in colour and smelling a little of almonds! Fortunately the pink colour fades on drying.

The acrylic water is dabbed on to the wake with a flat brush a few square centimetres at a time. Using the airbrush as a small blowgun, the gel is blown into waves, while the air breaks up the gel, creating a very realistic-looking, foaming wave pattern.

To finish off the base for ORP *Orzel*, some flow from the pump vents is added with a little more cotton wool and acrylic gel. This time the cotton wool is pasted on to a piece of cellophane and left to dry. Once dry it can be peeled away and trimmed to size before being fixed in place with a little more acrylic gel.

A good water base is something that requires a little patience and practice to create, but getting it right means you can produce a really stunning model of a ship in its natural element.

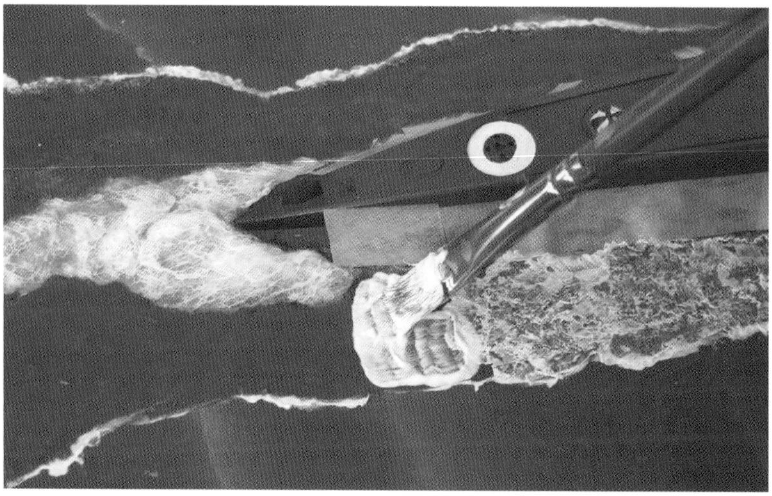

Dabbing on the acrylic water with a wide brush helps to create the start of the waves; the hull is masked off to prevent it blowing on to the paintwork.

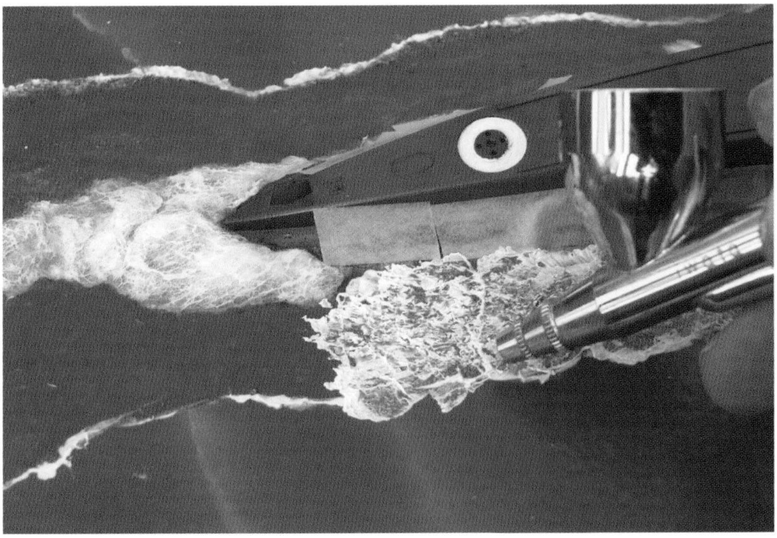

Quickly working over the acrylic water with the airbrush before it dries, a small area at a time, will blow it around and help it to look convincing.

Although submarines are much simpler than other types of ship, they can still result in a very interesting model.

Chapter Ten

Advanced Building – *Admiral Graf Spee*

SOME WAYS TO ADD EXTRA DETAIL

Every kit can in some way be considered as a starting point. With most, that point is quite a way down the slope; with others we might be lucky and will be much nearer the summit. Of course the way to determine the exact starting point is with reference to plans, photographs and any material that can provide reliable information. The increase in popularity of comprehensive upgrade sets means that many of the popular plastic kits now have an easy way of adding significant levels of detail all in one box. These generally include etched brass, replacement resin parts and turned brass barrels as standard, while some will include wooden decks.

The downside to these sets is that they are usually expensive, and it does seem that at times parts are replaced just for the sake of it. Care needs to be taken when using these sets, as the instructions may not correspond to the steps laid out in the kit, so it is easy to miss parts off. Continual reference back and forth between the kit and the upgrade set instructions is essential. Despite the minor drawbacks, there are some excellent sets available that will result in a very highly detailed and impressive model.

However, not all models have the luxury of a bespoke upgrade set, in which case it will be necessary with the help of reference to plans and photos, to work out which parts will be needed. There will in most cases be something available in the form of etched brass, turned barrels, anti-aircraft, radars and boats, but every now and then we may need to turn to a little scratch building to replace weak or missing parts.

THE ACADEMY 1/350 *GRAF SPEE* KIT

This chapter will focus on a build of the Academy 1/350 kit of the *Graf Spee*, an easily available and popular kit with only one rather expensive upgrade set to help out (assuming the standard version of the kit is the one purchased). There are only two etched-brass sets available, one from Eduard and the other from White Ensign Models; both have their merits, but on the whole the former was most suitable for the build of this kit, given that a number of the parts from the kit would be replaced.

A review of the kit using reference materials revealed that the light anti-aircraft weapons were a particular weakness and would need to be completely replaced. Veteran Models of Taiwan fortunately make some excellent 1/350 replacement parts, and a number of these sets are ideal for the *Graf Spee* model. These sets are a very good way of raising the level of detail since they include small items such as observation

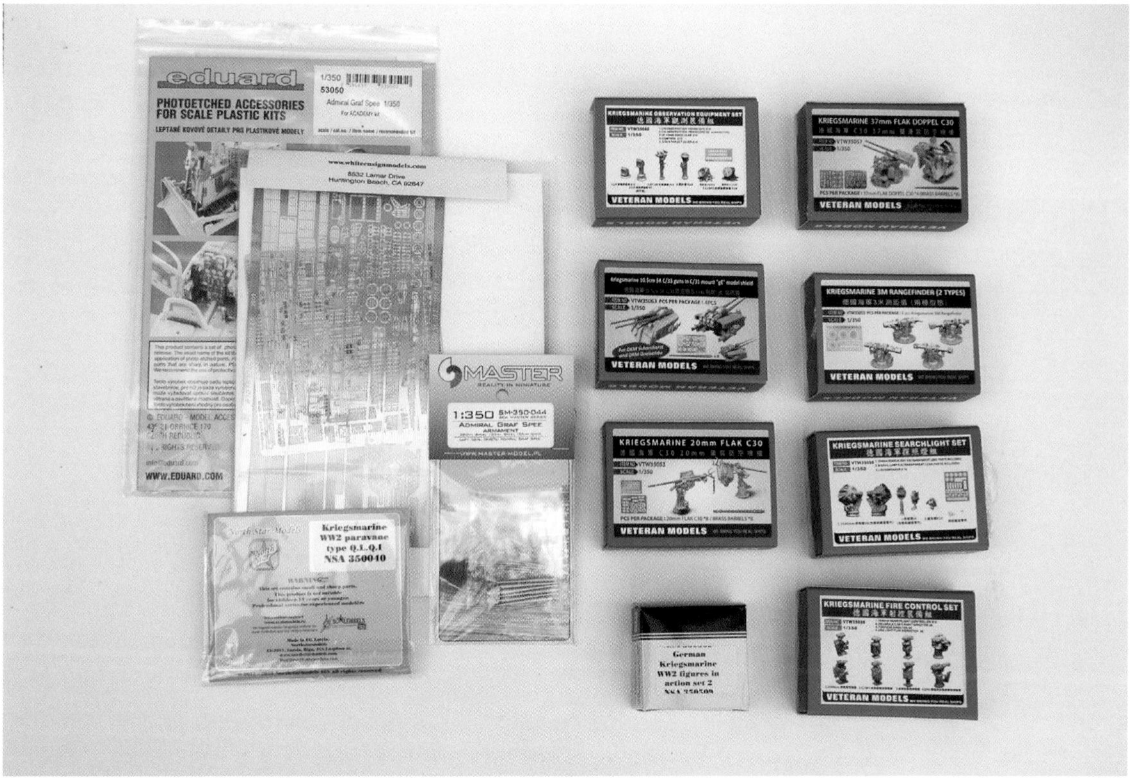

After-market accessories used in the Graf Spee *build, including various Veteran Models sets and etched brass, brass barrels and 3D-printed figures.*

equipment, rangefinders and searchlights, as well as the more obvious weaponry.

Choice of references is of course essential in determining where the base kit can be improved, and there is generally a good deal of choice, especially when building a popular subject. Look for those that have plans and details of the ship, as these will be the most useful; use these to assess the kit and see where it may be lacking.

Remember that every kit is just a starting point, and add your own stamp of individualism to your model by seeing what you can do to improve it. Ideally we would use original reference material, as of course every new interpretation runs the risk of error, but this is obviously not always possible, and sometimes we will have to make do with whatever is available. This is not to say that modern publications will necessarily contain errors, but using more than one source of information is a good way to prevent mistakes that have been made in a reference being repeated on your model.

Few will be fortunate though to have a library that covers all periods and nationalities, and buying reference material for every model can add considerably to the cost. In that case some compromise is needed, and choosing a couple of references may well be enough. Kagero publish a good range of informative books with plans, sectional drawings and 3D renders; similarly the series of books titled *Anatomy of the Ship* covers a number of subjects and contains a great deal of useful information. Shop around, but as always, you will find that books contain plenty of plans and photographs that will be most useful.

Some of the references used include the Top Drawings series by Kagero, which contain detailed plans and drawings.

THE HULL AND DECKS

With references in hand, the first task is to check through these, the kit and the etched brass sets to determine where the model will need to be altered, and where there may be errors that need attention. Quite often upgrade sets won't seek to correct mistakes, but will just add further detail to errors in the kit. This needs to be assessed and weak points noted to be addressed later in the build.

The Hull

First the hull will be assembled along with the decks, which brings us to the first job, as the kit is full hull with the option for waterline. In common with many similar kits in this scale, a recess along the waterline on the inside of the hull marks where it needs to be cut. For this a scriber is the best tool as it will remove a sliver of plastic with each pass, and is easier to control than a scalpel in this instance.

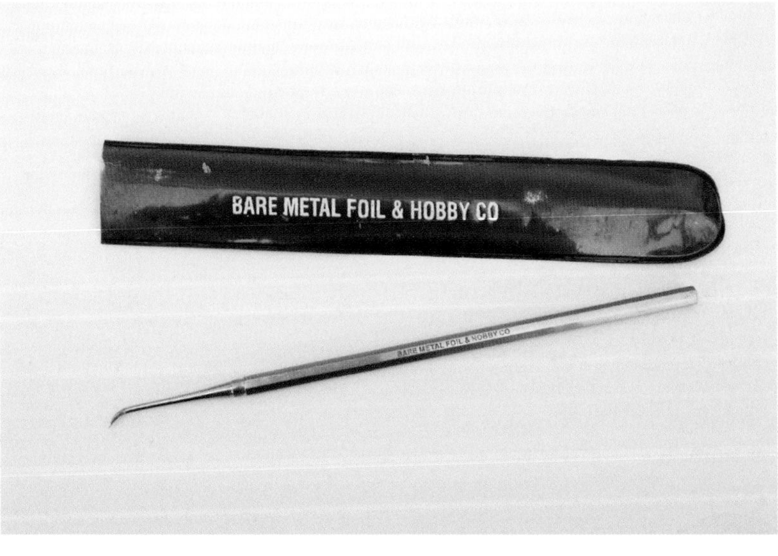

The scriber made by Bare Metal Foil is perfect for separating the 'above' and 'below' waterline sections of the model easily.

A waterline plate is provided with the kit, and the two halves of the hull are glued to it using masking tape to help set it in place. Whilst the glue is setting, check the fit of the main deck section to make sure the parts don't set with a gap.

When using upgrade parts it is often the case that we have to fill any location points intended for kit parts that are being replaced. As with the smaller holes meant for locating the railings, this can usually be done just with a little filler and sanding. Where the location points are larger, plastic rod of suitable diameter can be cemented into the hole and trimmed once dry to produce a clean finish.

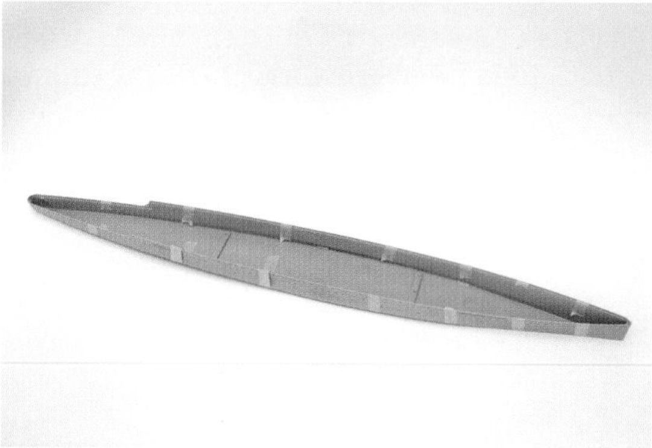

Using masking tape to hold the hull sides in place whilst the glue sets will prevent the parts from slipping out of position and creating problems later.

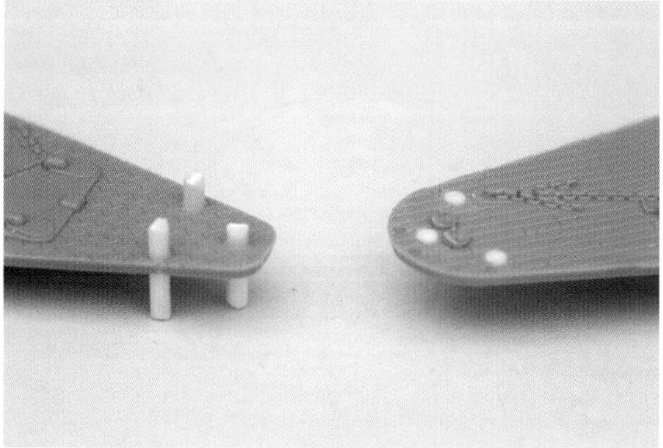

Having a range of plastic rod of varying diameters is very useful not only for construction, but also for filling larger holes in kit parts.

The Decks

It is not uncommon with larger-scale ships for decks to come in two parts, which almost inevitably will leave some sort of gap that not only has to be filled, but also rescribed if deck planking is featured. No design is perfect, of course, although perhaps if a little more thought had been given in this case the join could have been placed a few millimetres further along the deck where it could easily have been hidden under part of the superstructure, which spans the width of the hull. Still, this gives us the opportunity to see how this kind of problem can be resolved, as it is not unusual to find this on 1/350 injection-plastic kits.

First the gap needs to be filled with a hard filler – that is, not one that will crumble when it is scribed. Milliput is a good choice for this, especially if there is some width in the gap. In this case there was little in the way of a gap, so plastic filler was used, but allowed forty-eight hours to dry completely. Once dry it can be scribed using the same tool as used previously on the hull.

A guide is needed to keep the planking lines straight, and for this some label-making tape, such as that made by Dymo, is ideal. This is a very thick tape with a peel-off backing; the thickness of the tape helps the scriber stay straight, and it can be applied and reapplied several times as necessary. Simply run the scriber lightly along the edge of the tape a few times, making sure that the undamaged planking lines are followed.

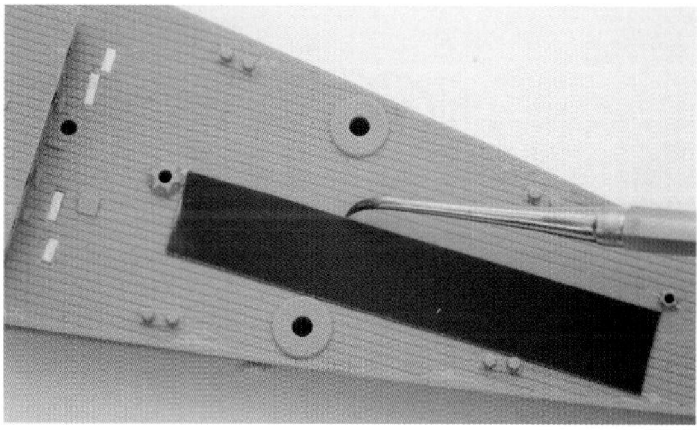

Ensure the lines of the planking are followed when applying the guide tape, and lightly run the scriber through these to reinstate the lines.

THE MAIN SUPERSTRUCTURES

Attention now turns to the main superstructures, starting with the lower platforms and decks, of which there are two main parts, fore and aft of the boat stowage. These are first test fitted to make sure they will sit neatly on the main deck, since the plan is to build and paint the superstructures separately and add them to the main hull and deck for final assembly. On checking the kit parts once assembled, it was found that the sides of the rear deckhouse had turned inwards after assembly; this can sometimes happen due to the action of polystyrene cement, which essentially melts the parts together. Using the digital callipers, the correct distance can be measured, and a piece of tube cut to the exact length can be inserted between the two side walls to re-establish the correct distance. Run some thin cement around the join to hold it in place.

With the plans and drawings in hand, the superstructures can be altered and detailed as necessary, using the etched brass details. Starting with the forward superstructures and first checking for differences between the kit and drawings, a few errors are spotted. The most significant of these – although it is something that often goes unnoticed – is that the deck on the lower section is shown as entirely planked, when in fact the forward part should be steel covered. Some filler and a little sanding is needed here to remove the engraved planking to leave a smooth surface.

Other changes include removing the inaccurately shaped boat supports, and scratch-building these from square-sectioned plastic. A good way to get parts such as these identical is to tape two sections together when cutting, so that lengths and angles are the same. The same approach is used to make the missing vents alongside the

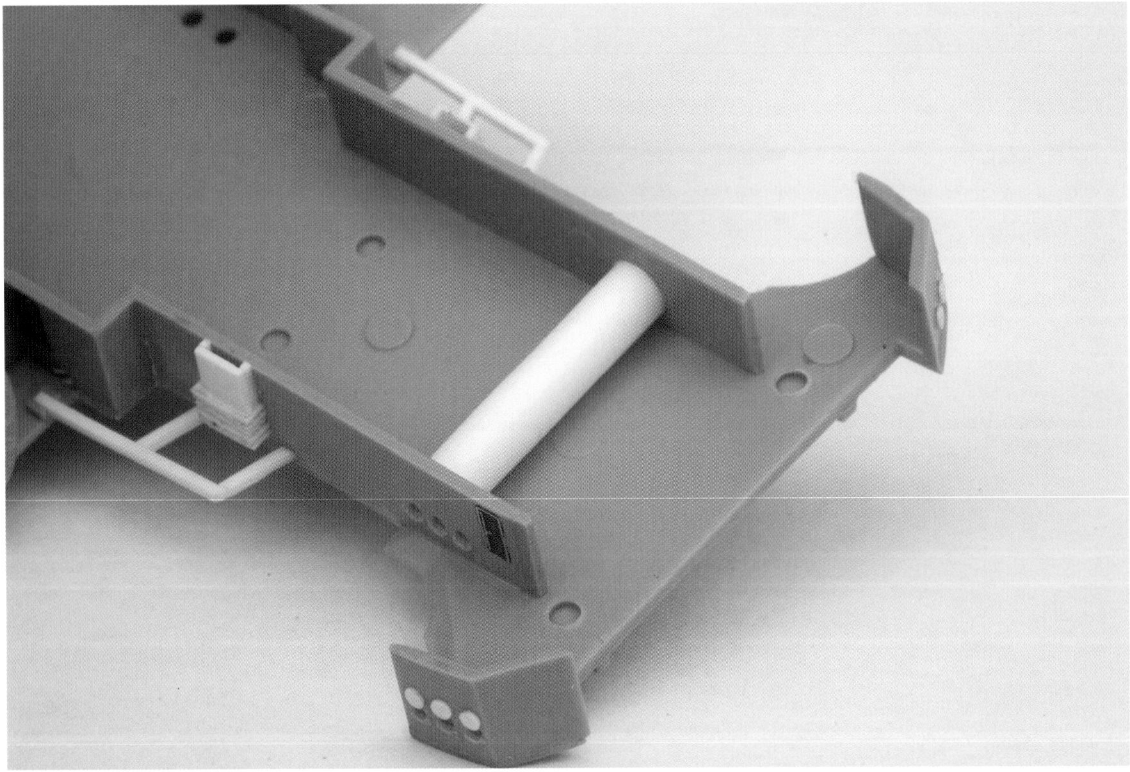

Any misalignments with parts that should be vertical can be corrected by inserting a section of plastic tube to regain the correct 90-degree angle.

superstructure, where alternate lengths of smaller and larger strips of plastic cut to size can be sandwiched together to create this detail, with a thicker strip sanded down around the edges to create the angled cover.

A slightly raised platform for the funnel is missing from the kit; this is very easily made with a little plastic card.

Another detail added is the porthole covers, unfortunately missing in the etched detail sets. These are made from thin plastic card or paper, in this case with a punch and die set. This is an expensive tool, but if it is looked after, a well-made set, such as the one from RP Toolz, will last a very long time. An alternative is to thinly slice plastic rod, which can work well with a little practice.

The forward section of this superstructure is quite incorrect on the kit: a small deckhouse supporting one of the rangefinders is both the wrong shape and too high. Unfortunately this means that the rangefinder once in place will also be too high and will block some of the bridge windows behind it. By contrast the armoured observation house in front of this is too low, and needs to be raised. The rangefinder house from the kit is first removed with the razor saw, and a new part is scratch-built from plastic card and rod.

This kind of shape, narrower at the rear than the front and bulged at the sides, is typical of the difficult shapes found on ships, and is a challenge to recreate successfully by eye. A scaled set of plans

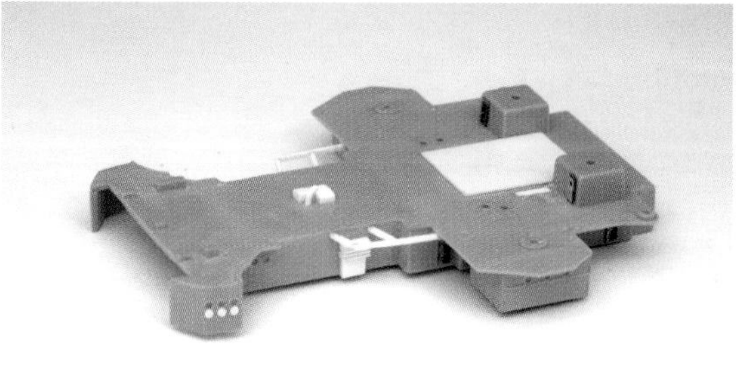

Good references are essential when adding detail to the model; upgrade sets will only go so far to do this, and going further can be a very enjoyable part of modelling.

The extra details added by the etched-brass upgrade set, some scratchbuilding, and more generic etched hatch-cover parts give much more interest to this area.

is very helpful in producing this, since they can be copied, cut out and stuck to some plastic card, then cut out to give the shape needed. More plastic card cut to shape using the observation house part as a template is used to fill the gap in the deck, along with filler to create a smooth base.

The last adjustment to this part is to add more plastic card to create the step at the rear of the housing, as it needs to be levelled off with the slightly higher open part of the observation deck. Shields at the rear of this are made from 15-thou plastic card, since those in the kit are both poorly shaped and too thick.

THE BRIDGE AND CONNING TOWER

Perhaps the most easily identifiable feature of *Graf Spee* is the large, almost pyramid-shaped bridge and conning tower. This attracts attention, which makes it worth investing in a little extra effort to detail. Overall the kit part is good, although lacking in detail, much of which can be added using the etched upgrade sets in the form of doors and hatches. Triangular supports for some of the platforms are provided, but they have not been included in either the Eduard or White Ensign sets for the lower and larger platform. These can be made by hand from offcuts of brass, but a simpler method is to use paper infused with CA adhesive, which has the advantage of being easily cut and folded so that the shape can be identical.

Making Identical Supports

When making the commonly used triangular supports for platforms, it is important to get these all the same, as any irregularities can be easily spotted and will spoil the effect. Although other materials can be used, paper is the best for this as it folds easily and will hold a sharp edge.

First squeeze a few drops of CA adhesive on to some paper and spread it out, leaving it to harden; this will only take a few minutes. If there is a rough surface, smooth this down with some wet-and-dry paper.

Work out the required length of the part, and cut the width of the paper to this; then fold the paper in half lengthways. Now measure the height needed of the part, and fold the paper back on both sides to this measurement; this can be done as often as needed, but three folds will give four parts.

Open up the paper so that the edges of the middle fold can be used as a guide to trim off the excess, leaving the four sides of paper the same size. Now cut the angle of the part first, which should be from one corner to the opposite one, by holding a flat scalpel blade across it and pressing down until the cut is made.

Now cut out any lightening holes, ensuring the paper is held down firmly to prevent it slipping. The final cut required is to unfold the paper and separate the parts along the fold line.

Fold the paper accurately so that the parts will be the same size once cut; just start again if you make a mistake – it's only paper.

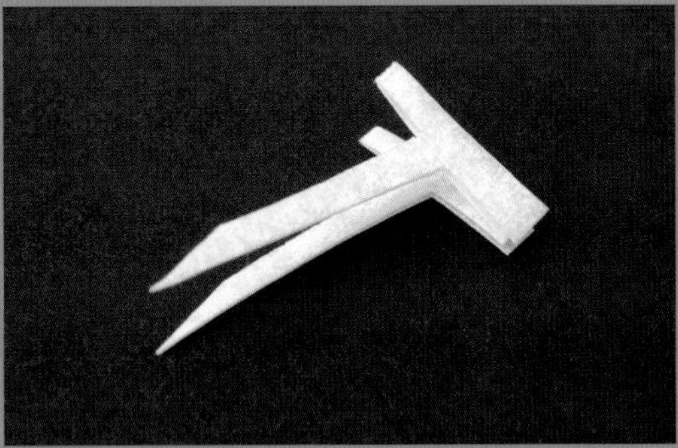

With some accurate cutting and folding you will have the basis for four identically sized parts.

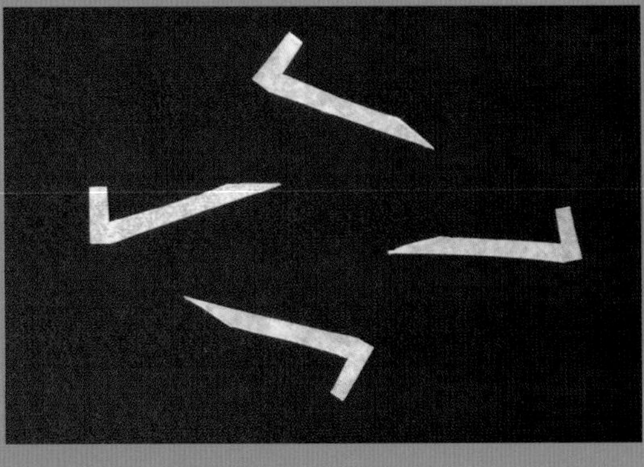

Keep the parts together when making the final cuts, using a little masking tape if necessary, to ensure that they all turn out identical.

Replacing the Footrails

By far the most challenging part of detailing the tower is replacing the moulded-on plastic footrails that are placed around it at varying levels. The kit parts could be left, but they create a question in the viewer's mind as to what they are intended to represent, so although it is a task requiring some patience, it is worth making the improvement in this area to raise the level of detail and realism.

First the kit parts are removed with the microchisel, and lines drawn around the tower to indicate where the replacement parts should be. For the footrails, the IJN handrails set from Five Star Models is used; this provides a good number of suitable etched parts, so there are plenty to make up for the inevitable mistakes. Some accurate cutting and placement with very small amounts of thick CA adhesive is needed for this type of task; it is a demanding job, and one of those best done a section at a time as this will help with accuracy. The finished result is certainly worth the effort, as it adds a lot of finesse to the most noticeable area of the model.

A similar treatment is required for the funnel, along with some pipework in the form of brass wire bent into shape. More supports are required under the main platform, along with ammunition boxes for the light anti-aircraft weapons. A simple but effective additional detail on this part is to drill out the solid exhaust vents and add some plastic rod to the underside to simulate the funnel pipes.

Piping can be made with brass rod by bending one part to shape and leaving this long to be taped to the cutting mat. Bend the rest around this, and cut to size.

Back and front views of the main bridge and conning tower; most of the platforms have been left off to simplify painting.

THE MAIN AND SECONDARY ARMAMENT

The Gun Turrets

As supplied, the kit turrets are quite bare and contain some inaccuracies. For some reason there is an odd chevron of plastic on the angle front of the roof, which seems to bear no relation to anything. This is easily removed with the scalpel, as are the heavily moulded access ladders on each side. The turret wings are misshapen, and a little more scratch-building is needed here to achieve a more acceptable part. A few sheets of thicker plastic card, laminated then carved and sanded to shape, form these parts.

With a complex shape such as this – a flat front, and rounded rear and side – the best way to get a uniform shape for all four parts is to first ensure that the starting rectangle shape for each part is identical. These can then be shaped with a sanding stick, working on each part sequentially until completed. There is more chance of uniformity this way than by finishing one part entirely and trying to match the rest to it.

Rivets are a feature of the actual turrets, and these are absent from the kit parts. Adding these creates a nice armoured feel to the turret, and is done quite easily with Archer rivet decals. Those intended for 1/72 vehicles are most suited to this scale. They are used in the same way as any other decal, although they do need to be carefully cut into strips and placed using setting solution. Once painted over lightly they give a very pleasing look to what would otherwise be quite a plain turret.

The Gun Barrels The main feature of the gun turrets is, of course, the gun barrels themselves, and the plastic kit parts can be replaced with very nice turned brass examples from Master Barrel. Fitting these does require a little surgery, first by removing the mountings for the kit parts with the micro-chisel and cleaning up the area. *Graf Spee* did not have blast bags, which help to hide the mounting of the barrel, so this needs to be done cleanly and accurately. A section of plastic tube cut to the correct width and then reduced to the required height is the starting point. Place this into the opening of the turret, holding it in place with a little Blu Tack. The points where the holes need to be drilled to accept the barrels can now be marked. Remove the plastic section and drill out the holes for the barrels, then glue this back into position.

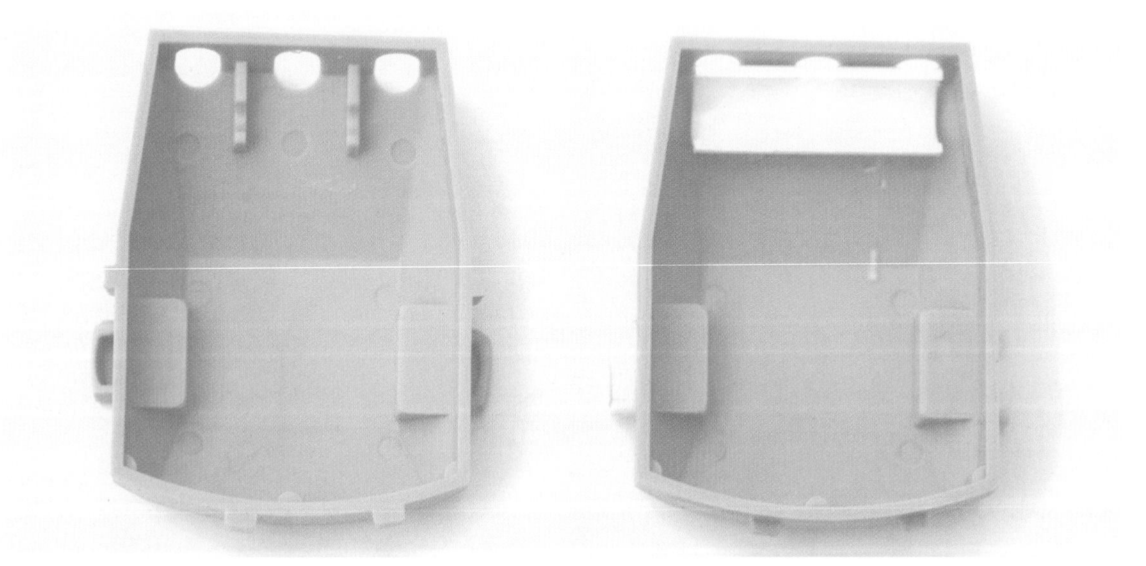

Brass barrels need a solid support to ensure they do not sag under their own weight; use plenty of adhesive on the inside of the mount once in position.

There will be a small stub at the rear of the barrel, so the drilled hole only needs to be big enough to accept this. The barrels can now be inserted into the hole and glued into place with CA adhesive. Position the middle barrel first and let this set in place. A good way to ensure that all the barrels are at the same angle is to then hold the turret in place on the cutting mat with some Blu Tack, then do the same for a piece of plastic rod placed under the barrel. The remaining barrels can then be positioned using the rod to keep them all at a uniform height.

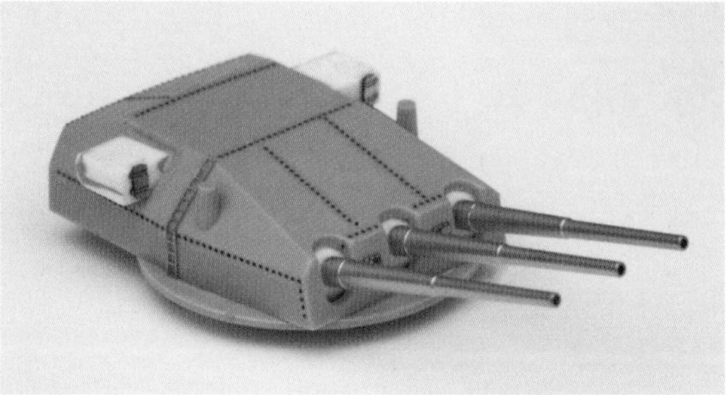

The completed turret showing the scratchbuilt wings, rivet detail and the addition of brass barrels to make a far more detailed and accurate part.

The Secondary Turrets

As with the main armament, the secondary turrets benefit from a little etched brass and a turned brass barrel. These are open to the rear, and a breech block must be made to take advantage of the etched back plate. A slice of square plastic rod drilled out in the centre, then notched on one side, serves as the breech block.

Although not a part with much detail, the secondary turrets are improved with photoetched rear doors, a scratchbuilt breech and a brass barrel.

Anti-Aircraft Guns

Lighter weapons are often an area where replacement rather than upgrade is needed, largely due to the limitations of plastic moulding, which results in barrels that are too thick and shields that are too heavy. The availability of parts depends on the subject, but there are plenty of generic sets available to cover most of the common weapons. In most cases these are in the form of resin accessories, often with etched brass details and brass barrels, such as the sets available from Veteran Models. Recently some outstanding 3D-printed parts are becoming more available, and are better priced than previously; these have the advantage of being mostly complete and requiring little assembly.

Graf Spee carries three types of anti-aircraft weapon: heavy 105mm, medium twin 37mm, and light single 20mm guns, all of which are available from Veteran Models sets and are excellent replacements. In the case of the heavy mounts, the kit parts are so lacking in detail that although etched parts are provided in the Eduard set, this would still leave much to be desired. The difference that is made by replacing the parts entirely with the Veteran sets is obvious from the photographs.

Regarding sets such as Veteran, in most cases they consist of some very small etched brass parts that are a challenge to put together, but given the slight increase in detail that these provide over the main components, the modeller can really make their own choice as to whether these are needed or not. Sometimes it is better to leave out very small and difficult parts altogether, rather than potentially spoil an already satisfactory assembly by trying to add that little touch of gloss on top.

The smaller 37mm and 20mm weapons are complex little models and require some patience to put together. With these types of miniature kit it is best to start with the base part and mount this on to some double-sided tape on a wooden craft stick, as this will leave both hands free to hold and position the very small parts. A slower-setting CA or epoxy is best for this type of work, but make sure when positioning parts such as the brass barrels that these are kept straight whilst the adhesive sets. Very small etched brass parts,

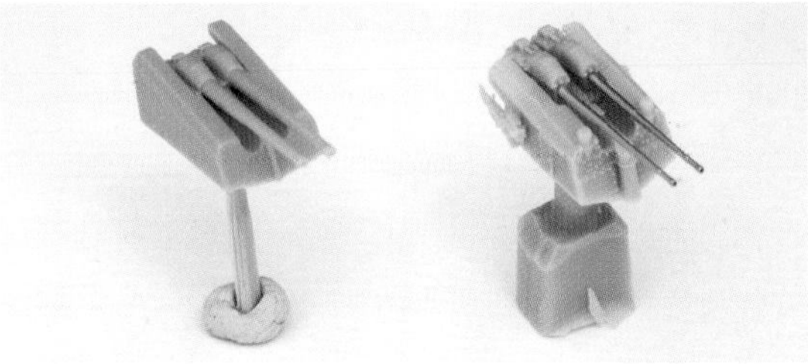

Comparison of the kit parts for the heavy AA weapons and the completed Veteran parts; there is a leap in terms of the amount of detail the upgrade set brings.

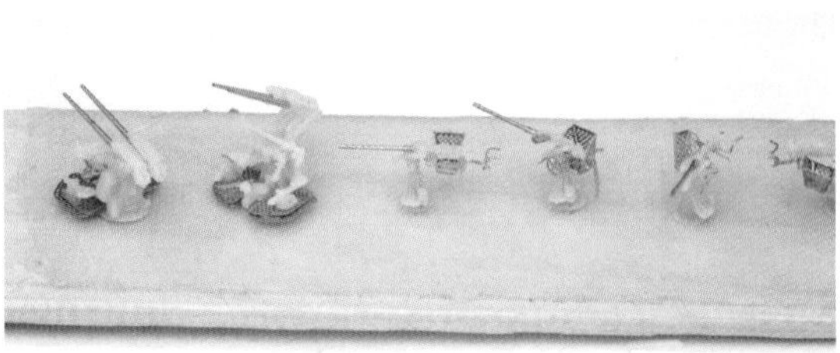

Some of the light AA weapons built from the Veteran sets; the finished results very much reward the effort involved.

should you choose to use them, can be attached with thinned PVA or even gloss varnish, which will be sufficient to hold such very light pieces.

SMALLER DETAILS AND ASSEMBLIES

By giving the same attention to the smaller details, a consistent level of workmanship can be achieved across the model. It is frustrating at times to see a completed model where a lot of effort has been put into some areas whilst others have been neglected. This includes details such as boats, rangefinders, searchlights, aircraft and the various other fixtures and fittings found around the ship. Many of these smaller parts can be found in aftermarket sets, and for World War II German subjects, Veteran Models again provides a number of these parts. There are, however, many options available, and it is more likely that a particular need will be met by at least one company, rather than having to resort

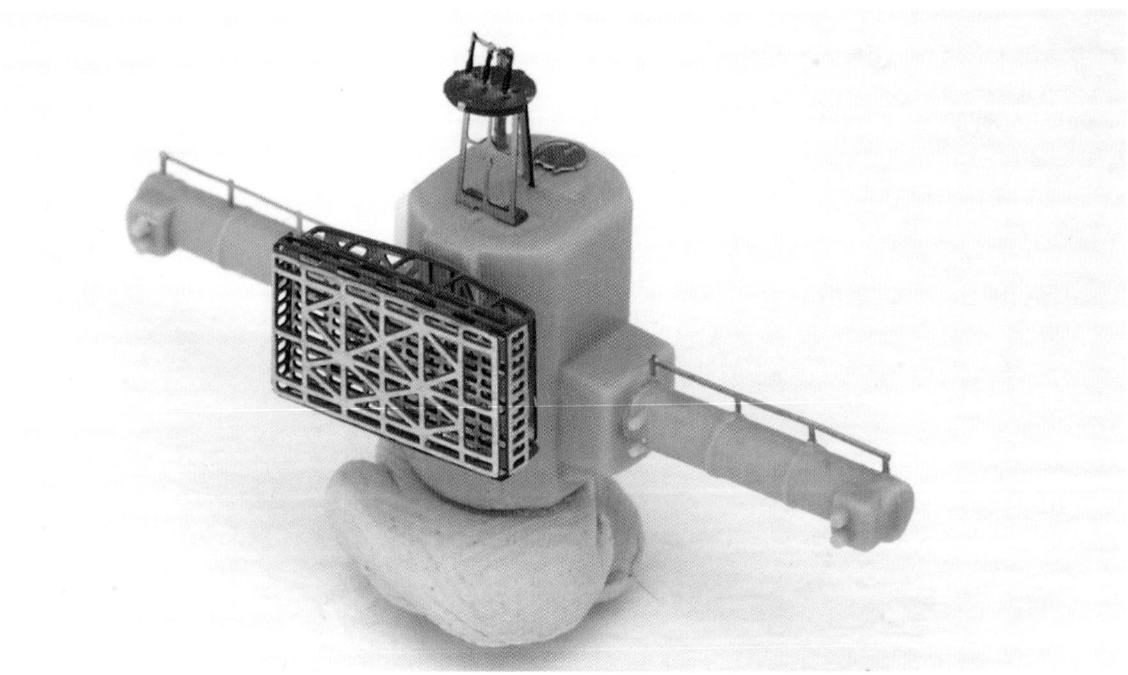

The main director detailed with the Eduard photoetched parts is a great improvement on the kit piece.

to scratch-building. And it must be said that for the modern modeller, being able to make those essential parts him- or herself is less of a requirement when so much is readily available – though perhaps this may be considered a mixed blessing.

Ship modelling can occupy a lot of time, and sometimes it may seem as though the completion of the model never gets any closer. Having well detailed and readily available upgrades certainly helps to reduce some of the repetitive elements, and if using these prevents the model being put on the shelf to gather dust, never to be completed, then the extra expense involved is surely worth it.

Once again Veteran provides some very helpful sets, which can all find a place on a model of *Graf Spee*, in the form of rangefinders, searchlights, fire control and observation equipment. The last three of these include a number of additional small items, which are a great help in adding detail around the model. Many of these are available in other forms, but having a number of items in one package is very useful. Of course references are needed to work out where all these various small items should be positioned. Four different types of rangefinder are placed around *Graf Spee*; these would have been used to control the main, secondary and anti-aircraft weapons, with the smaller versions for directing torpedo fire. The etched parts are good but don't go quite far enough, so a little additional scratch-building is needed to add the final details.

The Arado Floatplane

One of the most prominent features of the ship is the Arado floatplane; it sits high on the catapult amidships, and in its wartime camouflage provides a contrast to the rest of the model. It is obviously therefore worth investing a little time in this area, with the etched parts providing most of the detail. Since the aircraft has a simple and angular canopy, this can be replaced with some clear plastic sheet; so the canopy is removed, and a little work with the chisel and scalpel can hollow out the cockpit for some detail to be added. Even simple seats from plastic card are enough in this case to flesh out the cockpit.

Wings and control surfaces are scraped down with the scalpel to thin these down before a little detail is added to the engine cover. This features some raised oval shapes around the cowl, although the kit is entirely smooth. To represent this, some appropriately sized plastic rod is sanded on both sides until an oval is formed. This can then be sliced into sections and glued around the cowl; it doesn't matter if these are not the same thickness, as once in place and dried they can be sanded so they are all the same. Etched parts finish off the aircraft ready for painting, which is done before the canopy is added.

The Arado 196 floatplane as used on *Graf Spee*, and many other German capital ships of the period, has a very angular canopy, which provides an opportunity to add a layer of detail. Using some clear plastic from food packaging, two sections are cut to size and then bent to form similar U-shaped canopies. The first is glued into place using PVA and left to dry, and the canopy framing then painted using a small brush. Any smudges on this can easily be removed from the clear plastic with a wooden toothpick.

With a feature of the model such as the floatplane, it is recommended to spend a little more time on detailing the kit parts.

The finished aircraft: it is worth the effort to improve the look of what will be a part of the model that attracts the eye of the viewer.

Once dry, the second section is placed partly covering the first, to show the canopy open. Fortunately the windscreen is also a simple shape, made from another piece of the clear plastic, trimmed to size and continually test fitted to get the angle correct. Once all the canopy frames are in place they are painted again, and decals added: the aircraft is then complete.

Boats

As is not uncommon in many kits, scant attention has been given in this kit to providing a

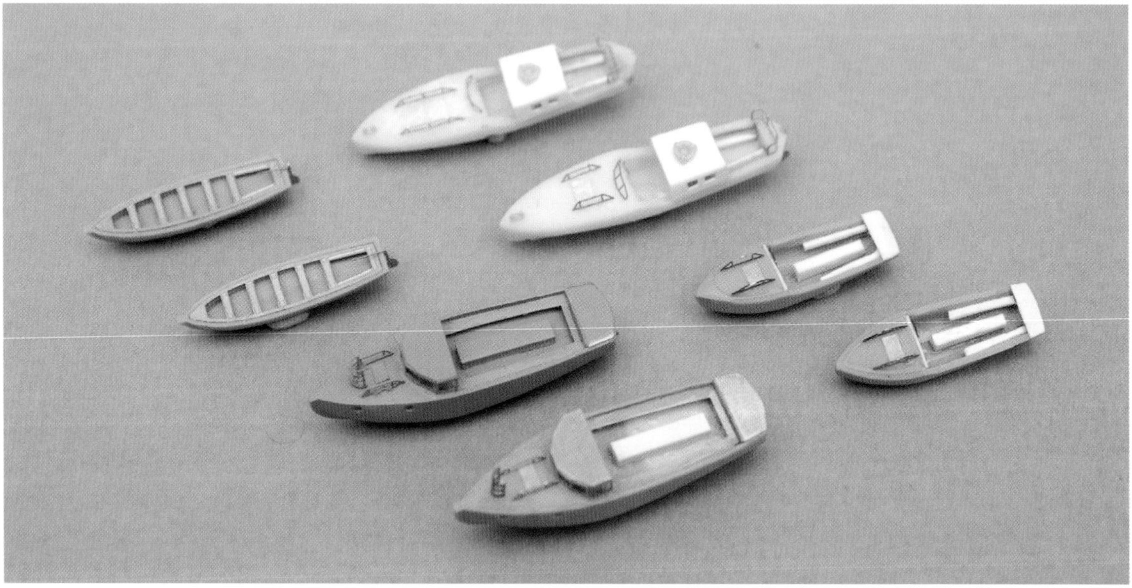

Photoetched parts and plastic strip combine to improve the look of the smaller boats; oars will be added after painting.

detailed and above all accurate representation. Failing to address this can be a real let-down on a model, and it often does need a little time and effort to rectify. Eduard provides some details to help, but as is often the case, some basic errors are not resolved. If the boats are very poor, it is always worth considering that at sea most would be covered with tarpaulin to some extent – this is particularly the case for open boats such as cutters and whalers. Some filler or white glue to cover over the boat can be a good option in this case. Motor boats can be improved by hollowing out the seating area and creating the seats from plastic card and rod. Once painted, these simple changes add greatly to the look of the finished articles.

PAINTING THE DECKS

More modellers are turning to laser-cut wooden decks for a quick solution to the challenge of creating a realistic-looking deck. Some of these can be very good, with the addition of washes to tone down the base colour, although all are additional and have to lie on top of the kit part. These are generally improving in quality from the initial rather rough-looking offerings, and can look effective, but on the whole it is somehow never quite convincing. Of course with so many kits available not every kit will have the luxury of this accessory, so for reasons of necessity or appearance, learning to paint a convincing wood effect is a skill very much worth learning.

The Lifecolor White Wood set is an easy way of getting variation in deck colours, with the Weathered Wood set used for darker decks.

A common misconception is that the decks of ships are a yellowish colour similar to freshly cut pine; in fact the teak from which they were often made would weather to a greyish tone over a short space of time. To replicate this we need to avoid the yellow and brown tones in the colour palette, and use more of the lighter greys and browns. An extremely useful shortcut to this is the White Wood acrylic paint set made by Lifecolor. This contains six shades of wood tones, ranging from a pale greenish colour to a pale brownish grey, which is ideal as a base colour.

With the superstructure sub-assemblies still kept separate, this base colour (UA779 Wooden Grey Umber) is first airbrushed on to the wooden deck areas to give a solid base coat. Using the other colours out of the pot would create too stark an effect, as there would be too much variation from the base colour. The first step, then, is to create a 75 per cent base colour with 25 per cent of the next darkest colour, in this case UA774 Old Peeled Deck. A mix of this, well thinned, is applied by brush on to the separate planks marked on the deck; a random pattern will be more realistic than one that is regularly spaced, so try and vary it, placing some of the same colour close together as well as further apart.

As this first mix is close to the base colour, a high proportion of planks are painted with this to create a slight variation from the base. The idea here is that there will be more planks closer to the base shade, graduating to fewer of those where the proportions of the base colour used in the paint mix is lower. In this way a variation in tone and colour is created without too much of an extreme of either the light or the dark mixes. We are aiming at a look that gives the impression of natural variation and weathering in the wood.

With the base colour airbrushed on to the wooden areas of the deck, we start to build up the effect of planking, with a slight variation from the overall colour.

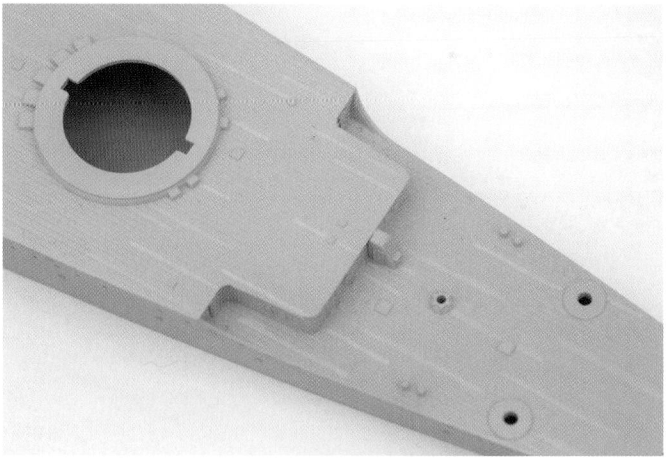

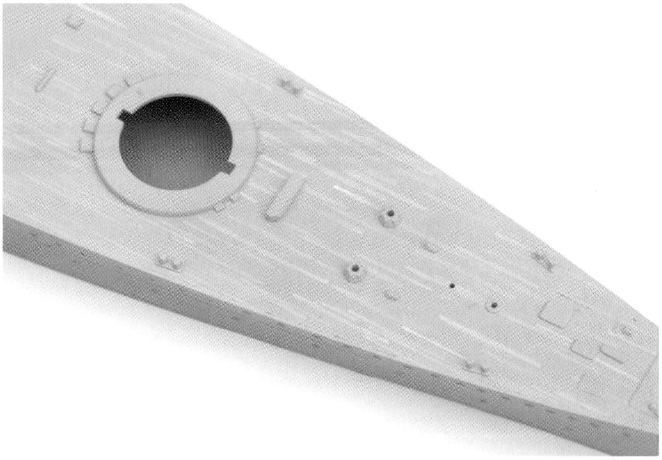

By mixing the base colour into the other colours in varying proportions a gradual change of tone and shade in the deck can be built up.

Next a 50 per cent mix of the base and second colour is made, and around half as many planks painted in this shade as with the previous mix. The final step for the second colour is to use a 75 per cent mix of this and the base colour, and half as many again as the previous step are painted in this mix. A thin mix of the paint also allows for some variation on the individual planks so they are not solid colour, something that also creates a less uniform effect. Of course a greater number of paint mixes than this can be used to create a very subtle gradation of tone.

The previous step is now repeated with the remainder of the colours in the set, with the lighter colours used more as highlights. Working through these will start to create a patchwork effect of shades and slightly different hues, since there are some green and pink tones in the set that are a good complement to the brownish colour of the base deck colour. Don't worry if this sounds like a long procedure, because it really isn't: since a relatively small number of planks are painted with each new colour, the effect we are looking for will quickly build up. If it appears a little too light at this stage don't worry, as the next step will tone this down and create a more subtle effect.

The final step is to blend the colours together by applying a wash over the deck. An enamel wash is used, in this case AK Interactive's Dark Wash For Wood Deck, which is a dark brown colour; however, any similarly coloured enamel or indeed

Continue mixing each new colour in similar proportions as previously, to build up gradually a patchwork effect over the deck.

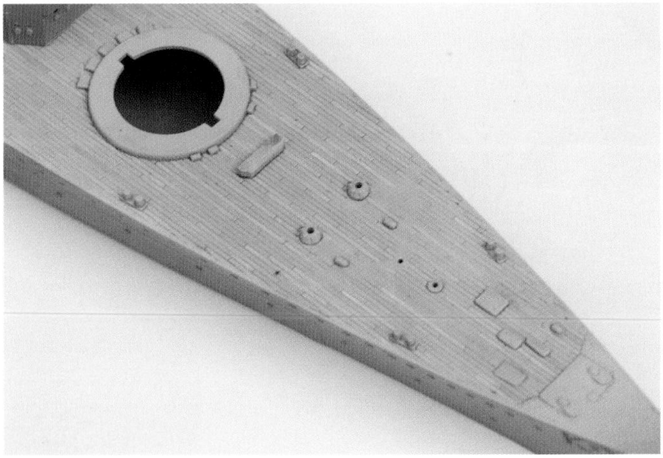

The wash helps to tone down the contrast between the lighter and darker shades, and emphasizes the planking by settling in the grooves.

oil wash would work just as well. In order to fill the gaps in between the planks to indicate the caulking, the wash is applied in several thinned-down coats with a flat brush, working at a 45-degree angle across the deck. This helps the wash to settle in the grooves in the deck. Leave each coat to dry before working across from the opposite side and at the same angle.

Although a black or dark grey wash would seem to be a better choice for indicating the caulking between the planks, this results in too flat a finish, and the contrast between planks and caulking is too stark. The brown wash blends the painted planks together and still allows for the lighter colours to remain as highlights to create visual interest, resulting in a very pleasing and realistic-looking deck.

PREPARING TO PAINT THE REST OF THE MODEL

Masking

With deck painting completed, we can start to move on with painting the rest of the model – but first the hard work of the previous step needs to be preserved by masking. It is much easier to mask a flat deck than superstructures, so it is usually advisable to paint the deck first and mask that, rather than the other way round. Use a good quality masking tape such as Tamiya, rather than the cheaper copies; they may look the same, but the adhesive on the tape is not as good, and there is a much greater risk of damaging the paintwork when it is removed.

Start by working round the small details on the deck; not all of these have to be masked – if they are easy to paint, then don't waste time masking them, just paint them later. Cut the tape into small strips to go round these details; if the area to be masked is circular, work round it with the small strips and then cover the edges of these with larger pieces to make sure they are held down.

Work round the rest of the deck until all the smaller details have been masked, then use longer and wider pieces to cover the rest of the area. Overlap the tape over the deck edges, and trim these with a sharp blade. Continue until all the deck area has been covered, then move on to the superstructure areas previously painted.

Check over the masking before painting, and push down any tape that may have lifted – use a cotton bud to press it into the angles between the deck and the raised detail. Many ships would have carried camouflage schemes, and depending on the type of scheme, it may be better to try and mask, then airbrush, rather than paint by hand as with the earlier model of USS *Wasp*. Straight-edged schemes are often easier to mask and airbrush than hand paint, since it is difficult to get the edges straight.

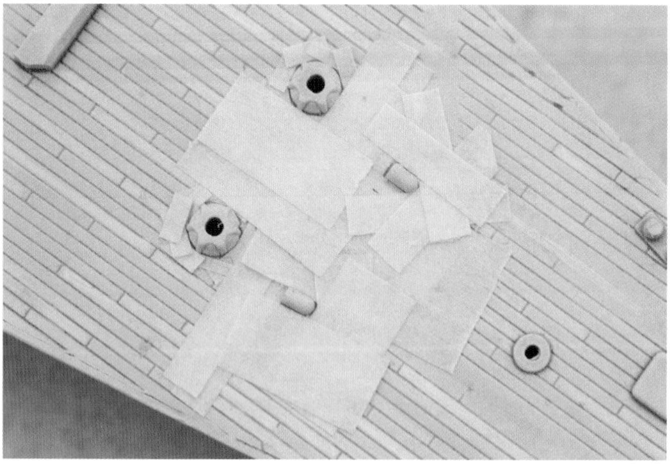

Masking appears to be a painstaking job, but it is really not that difficult – it is just a matter of using some simple shortcuts.

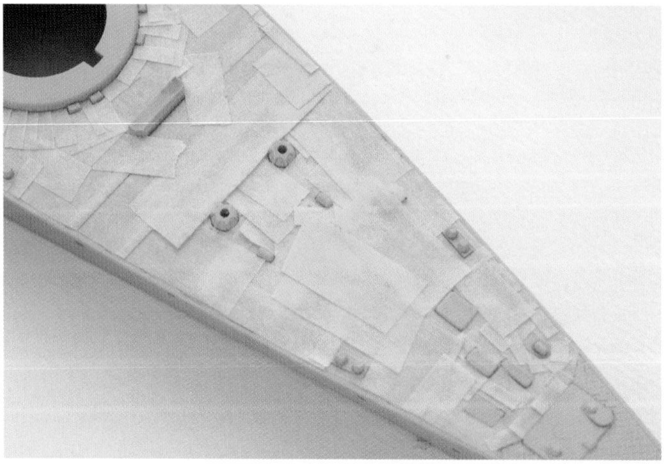

If there is a short period of time available between finishing the masking and doing the actual painting, go over the masks to make sure the edges have not lifted.

This type of masking is obviously more difficult, but the same principles apply as regards using small sections of tape to mark out the edges, which are then secured by larger pieces. When painting against masks of this type, remember to angle the airbrush from the tape side on to the area to be painted, as this helps prevent the build-up of a ridge at the edge of the mask.

One important thing when masking is to make sure that the tape is not left on too long; it is best to try and complete the painting quickly, within a few days, for example. If the masking is left on for a long time – meaning in the order of weeks rather than days – the adhesive on the tape can start to deteriorate and become gummy and even stringy when removed. The likelihood of removing the paint with the tape is then greatly increased, and it can be very difficult to restore the original paint job.

Pre-Shading

Pre-shading is a technique that will be familiar to aircraft and armour modellers, but it also has its uses when modelling ships. It can be used to break up an otherwise monotone hull or to create shade under overhangs on the superstructure, and is quite a simple technique. Patches of light colour, in this case a pale grey, are airbrushed in a random pattern on to the hull. The aim is not to show highlights, but simply to create some difference in tone once the top coat has been painted.

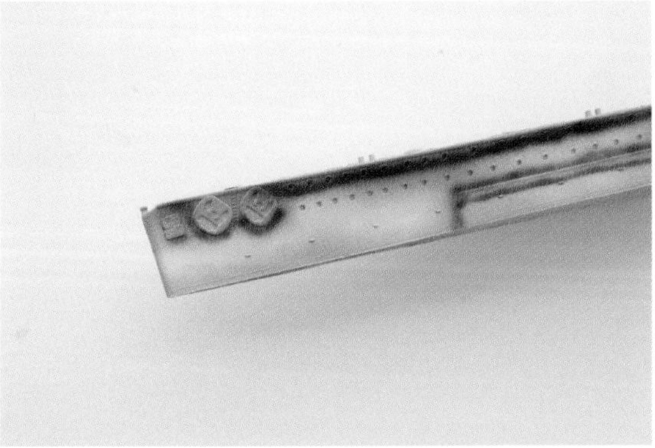

Use the airbrush freehand to mark out roughly the areas of light and the darker patches; if they are in the wrong place or too heavy, just cover with the top coat.

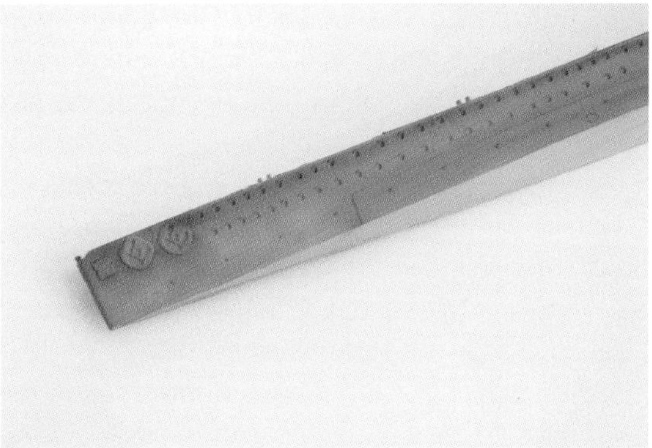

Build up the paint layers slowly to assess the progress towards the effect you want to achieve; this is almost complete.

Next a dark grey is used, but this time the aim is to create some shadow, so it is painted round the overhang of the hull, along the edges of the armour belt, and round the anchors. There is no need at this stage to be particularly tidy, so this can be done freehand with the airbrush, as any overworked areas can be covered later with the topcoat.

Similarly, areas under overhangs on the superstructure are painted with the dark colour to create the effect of shade, while the tops of the turrets are lightened with the pale colour. For the pre-shading effort to be effective it is important then to apply only thin coats of the base colour over this shading; if this is too heavy it will simply cover the pre-shading and any differences will be lost.

Thin the paint well, and apply with the compressor on a low pressure, gradually building up the coats of paint so that the underlying layers still show through. We want the pre-shading to add light and shade to the top layer so that it breaks up what would otherwise be a monotone block of grey.

MAIN PAINTING AND WEATHERING

With the model still left in sub-assemblies, the main painting can begin once the hull has been completed. The basic colours for *Graf Spee* in

1938, on which the model is based, are two shades of grey, with the hull slightly darker than the superstructure. Decks that are not wood are dark grey, and the open bridge area behind the fore turret is linoleum. Sovereign Hobbies produce their own range of highly researched and authentic enamel paints in their Colourcoats range, and also regularly release the results of their research free of charge on their website. Much of this research challenges the accepted information on paint colours, particularly those of the Royal Navy, so the most accurate paint matches are made available.

A very useful set for this model is a collection of eight pots specifically put together to cover the main requirements for *Graf Spee*. Although acrylics in their various forms have largely come to dominate the model paint market, there is still an important place for enamel paints. They do need longer to cure and are stronger smelling, but they are harder wearing so are much less likely to be worn off through handling, or removed along with the masking tape.

Painting proceeds largely as with earlier builds; in 1938, in the time period this model is shown, *Graf Spee* wore a simple medium-grey hull (Colourcoats KM02 Dunkelgrau 51) with lighter grey uppers (Colourcoats KM01 Hellgrau 50). On this occasion the ship is shown in peacetime when regular maintenance would be much easier, so weathering is kept to a minimum.

With the base colours applied, steel decks are painted with Colourcoats KM05 (Schiffsbodenfarbe III Grau I, a dark grey), this time hand brushed using a small, flat-bladed brush as this makes it easier to get straight edges where required. Some small areas covered in linoleum are similarly painted with Colourcoats brown enamel

Sovereign Hobbies Colourcoats range is an excellent brand of enamel paint and offers the most authentic matches currently available.

from the same set. This is all then treated with a couple of airbrushed coats of Alclad Acquagloss, to seal the paintwork ready for weathering.

This time weathering is mainly kept to the basics of shade, highlight and a little use of streaking wash round a few areas of the hull. First some thinned black oil paint is used to provide some depth around raised detail and shadow in angles of the superstructure. Many modellers choose to use a wash to achieve this effect; used heavily, this will result in the base colour being darkened, and it also has the tendency not to stay where it is wanted, instead spreading out untidily into the surrounding area and creating a watermark. Oil paint is ideal for carrying out this stage of painting since it can be removed with a clean brush dipped in turpentine or similar.

The main bridge tower of Graf Spee *with some shadowing and highlighting; the aim is to bring depth to the model without making the work obvious.*

Concentrating on the lower half of the raised detail to indicate shadow, the black is painted round the edge of the most prominent detail on the first pass. With the paint thinned a little more, it is then applied over the less raised detail, such as doors and hatches. This step is more akin to a wash, but is applied sparingly and only to selected parts.

Highlighting is achieved by using a little white to lighten the base colour, and painting the top edges of raised details to imitate light falling on to the model. The effect here is not the same as drybrushing, which is often overdone, resulting in all edges of surfaces being lightened to the same degree, which actually creates the opposite effect and makes the model look too flat and uniform. Keeping these last two stages to a minimum will create a more subtle variation of light and colour, which is most effective when it is almost imperceptible.

As often happens, it became clear at this point that the arrangement for handling the two cutters that lie between the secondary turrets was not only completely wrong in the kit, but had not been corrected by either of the two photoetched upgrade sets. The boats were slung from davits in between the paired gun mounts, so these needed to be made from scratch. As previously, to ensure an identical shape for the four davits needed and their brackets, four layers of 20-thou plastic card were laminated together, leaving a little over to allow for gluing together and also to make handling easier. These were cut and sanded into shape; once severed from the excess, the parts can then be assembled.

As a small variation, the boats will be shown on their davits ready for use, something warships often do when entering or leaving harbour. This does make for a fragile assembly, however, so these are left to the very final stages of completion once the model is mounted on the completed sea base.

One final piece of detail is to add a reflective backing to the excellent Veteran Models searchlights. This is made using tinfoil punched out with a RP Toolz large punch-and-die set, and glued into

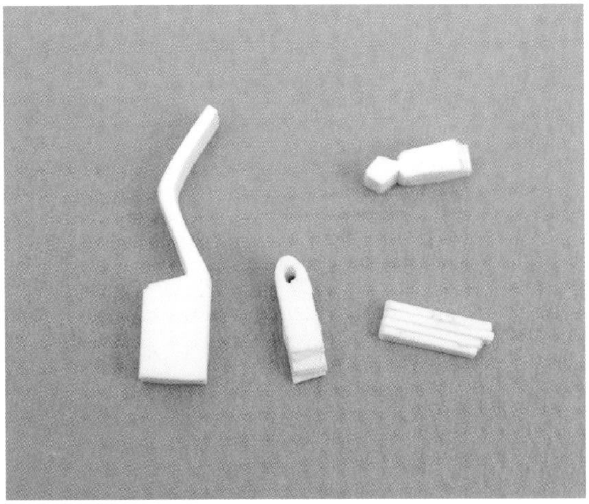

New boat davits made from plastic card; these are often supplied as photoetched, but are invariably too thin and not to scale.

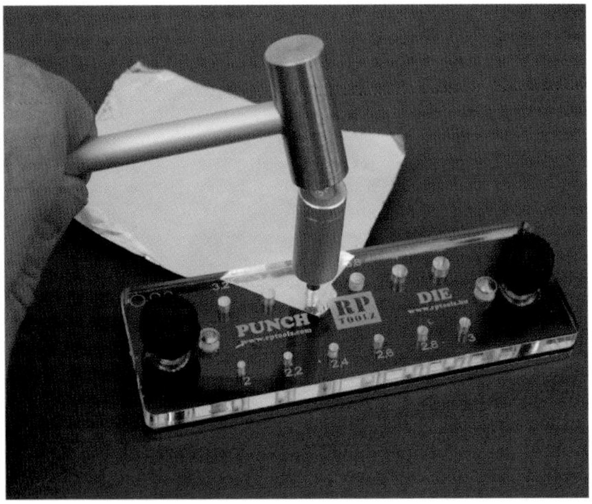

The Veteran Models searchlights are excellent replacements, but even these can be improved with a reflective backing.

The finished searchlights in place; as there are a number of these on the model they are an interesting detail.

place with PVA before the clear kit lens is added, then finished off with the etched protective screen. Although quite expensive, RP Toolz makes an excellent range of high quality modeller's tools that will last a lifetime as long as they are used and stored correctly. Particularly if you intend to do some scratch-building, these are really worth investigating.

FINAL ASSEMBLY

At this point we have the main sub-assemblies and small parts painted and ready to install, the deck painted and masking removed, the photoetch painted on the fret, and everything ready for final assembly and completion. The main aim at this stage is to work through the final assembly whilst ensuring there is no damage to parts already in place. For that reason anything that could potentially prove tricky to place, such as ladders and railings, apart from those around the deck edge, are installed first. Having etched railings that are designed for the kit are certainly a big help, but these still need to be fitted carefully so as to make the best use of them. Placing ladders first means that the correct spacing can be made so as to make sure the length of railing fits exactly. This is particularly the case where the ladders meet open deck areas, rather than fitting on to platforms.

Railings designed for a specific kit may not always be entirely correct; this is the case for the Eduard set, as the section around the midships 10.5cm gun mounts does not fit properly when folded and leaves gaps, since one element is too long. To amend this the railing is cut where it is overlong, and trimmed to size with nail scissors. Once the first section is in place, this can then be correctly positioned, taking care to avoid any gaps between the stanchion and rail. Should this happen, a little PVA can be used to bridge the gap, and painted later.

Very small parts, such as the details on the tower and open bridge, need to be added early on; these will require exact placement and a steady hand, with the temptation always to rest on part of the model whilst working. Of course, this runs the risk of damaging anything already in place, hence the process of working from the inside to outside of the model. Items such as the crane can have rigging added and then be left until last, as they will block access to the boat storage where precise alignment is needed. Similarly the large rangefinders are left off until the late stages.

Every model will be different, of course, in terms of how each part can be added safely, so as ever, plan ahead for best results. Stop at a suitable time to carry out some touching up of paintwork, as there will likely be some damage to parts, especially

Measure the distance of the railing section, then place one ladder in place, then the rail, then the second ladder; this makes sure there is no gap between ladder and railing.

Attention to the fit of railings greatly improves the look of the final model, even if it means a little extra work.

photoetched parts. Leaving this to the very end will once again risk damaging what is already in place. Gradually the model nears the final stages of assembly with all parts being put into position.

Everything is now ready for the final stretch towards completion – all remaining parts are added, along with some North Star 3D-printed crew figures to give the ship a sense of scale. It is tempting to spread the figures around the ship evenly spaced in the hope that this will have more impact, but that isn't how we as humans tend to interact. A much more realistic look can be achieved by using the figures in small groups, if possible giving the impression of some particular activity taking place, such as some routine maintenance, cleaning, being on watch, or simply leaning over the rails taking a cigarette break, as so many on-board photos seem to show.

Completing construction involves the deck edge railings; these are added almost last, as they can be very easily damaged. Masts are the final addition, to allow for rigging to complete the model. As always, care needs to be taken to ensure that masts are vertical and yardarms at 90 degrees to the centreline of the ship. *Graf Spee* has quite a complicated rigging scheme,

Many of the smaller parts, already painted and weathered, have now been added; this is a good point to go over and touch up any paint damaged during assembly.

3D-printed figures are a great improvement on the previous photoetched ones, but still need a little painting to add emphasis.

so there is an opportunity to use a number of different materials. First, brass rod and some scrap etch are used to add the various booms and stays around the main tower and funnel. *Graf Spee* has an unusual arrangement of signal flag rigging, with the main lines supporting these held out on booms, rather than the more usual attachment to yardarms. As this is likely to make a rather delicate structure, the horizontal lines are this time made with the use of the photoetched IJN mast rigging ring set made by Five Star Models; this can be used for any ship requiring a similar arrangement.

Sand-coloured stretched sprue is used for the signal halyards themselves, and this is glued to each side of the ring before tightening with an incense stick in the usual fashion. It is best to do a section at a time, tighten that, then move on to the next; trying to do it all at the end could lead to some lines getting too close to the heat source and melting. Yardarm rigging is with 0.1mm black-coated wire bent into appropriate curves; the remainder of the work is then completed with the same wire, stretched sprue or Uschi van der Rosten rigging line, depending on which is most suitable for the particular need. Insulators are made with a little white glue mixed with black acrylic paint and placed with a cocktail stick.

With the rigging complete the model can finally be attached to the sea base as before, and the water finished off using the methods we have already seen. Everything is now complete, and the model can be fitted into its purpose-built case and is ready for display.

With complicated rigging schemes a choice of materials is likely to be needed to give the best results.

The completed model, a suitable reward for the time taken and a superb display piece.

Setting the model in a base with plenty of space around it creates more of a feeling of the ship being at sea.

Chapter Eleven

Display and Photography

DISPLAYING THE FINISHED MODEL

After so much hard work to complete your ship model, it is worth spending a little more time to present it in the best possible way. Whether it is to be entered in a competition, shown at a show or club meeting, or something to be put on display at home, a well presented model is something to be proud of. There are two sides to presentation: the physical one, the base, and the display case and labels, and what is now almost entirely a digital one: photography.

Visiting model shows in continental Europe is an eye-opener in terms of how much care modellers take over the presentation not only of their individual models, but also of their model-club table displays. The pride taken over presentation to show the best that both the group and individual can do is evident, and investing a little time at this stage can turn your ship model into a real centrepiece to be proud of.

BASES AND CASES

A good solid and stable base will help preserve the model: something of inferior quality may warp over time and lead to the model being irreparably damaged. For a model built from a resin kit it is even more important, since especially if kept in a warm place, the resin may start to bend over time if not securely fastened down. A hardwood such as oak is a good choice for a small to medium-sized model, and this is a better choice than one made from ply or MDF due to the much more attractive look it provides. It can be drilled through and the model screwed to the base so that it is securely attached, then varnished to finish.

An oak base makes a very solid mounting for the finished model, and looks attractive when finished off with a little gloss varnish.

For very small models, bases intended for use for figure models are often something a little different and help to lend more of a presence. For the larger model a hardwood base is less practical as it becomes difficult to find the right size, and the cost starts to increase significantly. In this case some form of reinforcement will be needed in the form of wooden or metal strips or sections to hold the base flat.

Cases

More so than any other type of model a ship will attract dust, be vulnerable to damage, and be almost impossible to clean properly. After so much hard work, having the completed model protected by a case of some sort is a very good idea. There are basically three choices when it comes to these: an off-the-shelf acrylic case, a case in glass most likely made to order, or a case that you make yourself. The latter is likely to be the cheapest option, as even acrylic cases can become expensive as the size increases, especially if something has to be made to fit the completed model.

For this reason it is often a good idea to think of the case first, see what is available, and plan to build the model to the dimensions that can be bought off the shelf. This is generally possible for 1/700 and smaller 1/350 models, although when larger 1/350 ships are the finished product it becomes more difficult to find something to fit. Trumpeter makes a budget range of acrylic cases that are suitable for most but the very largest of models, and these are perfectly satisfactory if all that is wanted is a dust cover, since they are not the most attractive of display items. The problem with acrylic cases is that they will always have an injection mark on the top of the case that spoils the look, but more importantly they will wear quite easily over time and become scratched and stained. As a budget case, though, they are certainly a good solution.

When something a little larger or more refined is wanted, then the option is to purchase something custom built, or try to do it yourself. A custom-made acrylic or glass case will present your model in the best possible light; in the UK, Airframed is

Acrylic cases such as those made by Trumpeter are a good budget solution to keeping your model free of dust and damage.

The finished model of HMS Nadder *in a made-to-measure glass case makes for an item worthy of display at home.*

highly recommended as a supplier of glass cases built to any size needed. Should you be tempted to try a little DIY then it is possible to have glass and acrylic sheet cut to size. There is no substitute, however, for a professionally made display case that will give prominence to the finished model.

To complete the display, some form of label will provide a little information on the model and add to the finished piece. Many of the more popular ship kits will have something available already in photoetch, and these can be carefully painted to improve the look. Alternatively, companies such as Name It! in the UK will make bespoke labels in a variety of styles and sizes on self-adhesive metal backing. Whatever you choose, make sure it is spelled correctly!

PHOTOGRAPHY

Many of us increasingly use digital photography to share our model builds via social media, modelling forums or websites. This is a much more immediate means of communication than traditional magazines and books, and given that lower quality images are needed to ensure faster page-loading times, perfectly adequate photographs can be taken even with a decent mobile phone camera. However, even allowing for this, a few basic rules when taking photographs of your finished models will help to create a better impression and hopefully make the viewer linger a little longer to appreciate your work. These considerations also apply equally to those looking to use a digital camera to take something a little more studied and perhaps even for magazine or book submissions.

Background

First of all the background is important, and something plain that will not distract from the model is essential. A photograph with your cutting mat or workbench as a backdrop may be fine for something in progress, but for a completed model anything that distracts from the finished model will be a definite disadvantage. For small models a photocube is ideal, as these often come with a built-in light to help with filling in any shadows. However, as ships are long and thin, these quickly become too narrow, and a plain backdrop from card or a sheet is a good replacement.

Plain colours generally work best, and something white or pale will help to reflect light back on to the subject. Black makes for a dramatic photograph, but it will make any rigging invisible, so in most cases it is not suitable. Another alternative is to use a photograph of a seascape: print this out, usually in A3 size, and arrange it behind the model to create the appearance of a ship at sea.

Depth of Field

Good photographs can be taken even with a camera phone, although this will generally be limited in terms of the angles that will work. The main issue is what is termed in photography 'depth of field', which is the distance over which the subject will be in focus. For ship models this becomes an issue since their long and narrow profile means that it is difficult to keep much of the image in focus from certain angles. If you have only a simple camera or are using a phone, the lack of control means that for photographs to be fully in focus, it is only really possible from a face-on position, or close up. Taking a photograph from an angle will result in the image only being in focus for a small area around where the camera has focused, most likely leaving the bow and stern sections blurred.

This model of HMS Barham *uses a printed backdrop of a seascape to greatly improve the realism of the photograph.*

The problem of depth of field: only a small section of the hull is in focus, and both the bow and the stern of the model are blurred.

To take a photograph fully in focus over the whole length of the model, an SLR (single lens reflex) camera will be needed. At this point things become very technical and more the scope of a book on model photography by itself. For that reason we will keep to the basics of trying to get a decent photograph with simpler means. In most cases all that is needed is something that is good enough to show the model off to good effect for use on the internet. As discussed before, the first step then is to create a clear and uncluttered background that will not distract from the subject.

Light

Light is, of course, a major consideration. Photographs can be taken perfectly well in just daylight, although strong sunlight and shadows are to be avoided. A bright but overcast day is probably best; if the light is strong, this is when a photocube comes in useful, since it will prevent shadows but still allow sufficient light through. If not, a piece of card or sheet held up next to the model to block out the direct sunlight works well. When taking a photo in daylight is not possible, artificial lighting will be necessary, usually in the form of lamps.

The type of bulb used will affect the colour of light emitted, although not obvious to the eye: traditional tungsten-type bulbs cast an orange shade, LED bulbs vary from a yellow to an almost white light, neon is blue, and daylight bulbs mimic daylight. Your camera or phone will probably have a white-balance setting, and it is generally best to set this to auto and allow the camera to detect the difference. It is important, though, when using lamps to light a model, that the bulbs are all the same type, otherwise this will confuse the camera's sensor. If you plan to take a lot of photographs it is worth investing in a table-top studio set-up; this includes a folding box and lamps, and is suitable for smaller subjects.

Mobile Phones

Modern mobile phones have ever more sophisticated cameras built in, and these often have some settings that allow controls similar to compact cameras. These allow adjustment to shutter speeds, sensor sensitivity to light, white balance and other features to give the user greater control. It is worth making some test photographs with these settings on your phone and camera to see what difference they will make.

This is all very useful, but one main drawback of using a phone as your camera remains the difficulty of keeping it steady, since there is no means to attach it to a tripod for steadiness. Some help can be gained from steadying it on a nearby object, or using a small bean bag to keep it in position. For those interested in more than just some in-progress or finished snapshots, at some point progress to a more specialized piece of equipment is likely to be desired.

Taking Your Photographs

With the set-up ready to take photographs, bear in mind the depth-of-field issue when taking the images, and choose angles that will minimize the problem. Some improvement can be made by stepping back from the subject and taking the photo from around 18in (45cm) away. This allows more of the length of the model to be in focus. If the camera has an option for image size and quality, always set this to the highest factors since this will help retain the image quality should any editing be required.

Make sure to take plenty of photos using different angles around the model and also at differing heights, as well as with varying camera settings. Any that do not work out can be easily deleted, leaving a set of images to work with. Ideally download these on to a laptop, as even the most basic of image viewing software is likely to have some editing facilities so photos can be cropped or straightened, or brightness and colour altered.

A table-top studio is an inexpensive way of getting a clean background, with lamps and diffuser screens to stop harsh shadows.

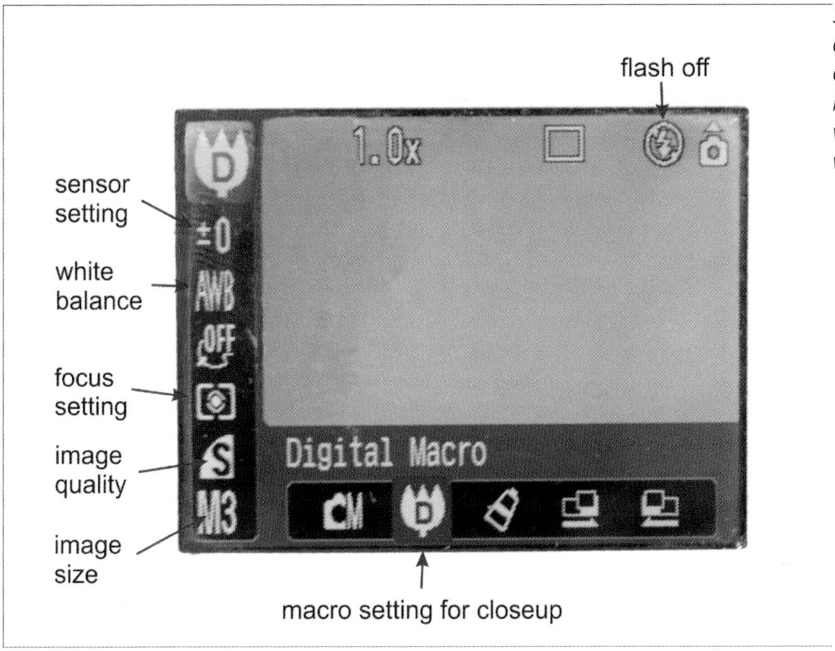

Settings on a typical small digital camera give greater control over the final image; take some time with the manual to learn what these are.

By following these few basic principles you should end up with photographs that will do your model justice, and create a good impression wherever you choose to share them. Of course this can all be taken much further, and model photography may become an important part of the hobby itself – but that is a much more complex area than can be covered here, and is the subject of another book!

MODELLING IS A SOCIAL HOBBY!

Before the internet became an everyday part of our lives, modelling was mostly a solitary hobby only interspersed with club meetings for those close enough to a club to be able to join, or occasional model shows. We are fortunate today in being able to connect with like-minded people almost anywhere in the world, even if we may never meet face to face. Of course this means it is much easier to hear about new developments and products, discuss questions and gain answers to problems, and generally spend time communicating with others who share the same interests.

There are a number of forums dedicated to ship modelling, and social media has very many modelling and historical groups that provide sources of information. Here you can show your work and request constructive criticism – often others will notice something that could be improved. There will always be somebody with a higher skill level – although modelling should not be seen as a competition: yes, of course there are competitions, but first and foremost it is a hobby to be enjoyed, and however that happens is absolutely fine.

Getting to know fellow modellers is a highly rewarding experience, even more so when they are from other parts of the world and from entirely different cultures. It is fascinating to see how very different we may all be, but also how there is still a great deal of similarity and common ground when we share the same interests. Enjoy your modelling.

Index

RELATED TITLES FROM CROWOOD

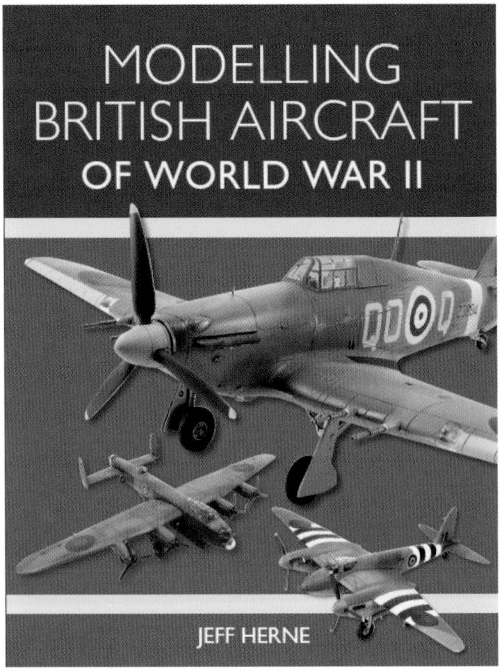